CHINA'S MARKET COMMUNISM

China's Market Communism guides readers step by step up the ladder of China's reforms and transformational possibilities to a full understanding of Beijing's communist and post-communist options by investigating the lessons that Xi can learn from Mao, Adam Smith and inclusive economic theory. The book sharply distinguishes what can be immediately accomplished from the road that must be traversed to better futures.

Steven Rosefielde is Professor of Economics at the University of North Carolina, Chapel Hill and a member of the Russian Academy of Natural Sciences. One of the world's leading experts in Soviet/Russian Studies, Comparative Economic Systems and International Security, he is the author of numerous books including *Asian Economic Systems* (2013).

Jonathan Leightner teaches at Augusta University in the United States and Chulalongkorn University in Thailand. Johns Hopkins University hired him to teach at the Hopkins-Nanjing Center in China for 2008–2010. His publications include articles on China's trade, exchange rates, foreign reserves, fiscal policy and land rights.

CHINA'S MARKET COMMUNISM

Challenges, Dilemmas, Solutions

Steven Rosefielde and Jonathan Leightner

Routledge
Taylor & Francis Group

LONDON AND NEW YORK

First published 2018
by Routledge
2 Park Square, Milton Park, Abingdon, Oxon OX14 4RN

and by Routledge
711 Third Avenue, New York, NY 10017

Routledge is an imprint of the Taylor & Francis Group, an informa business

British Library Cataloguing in Publication Data
A catalogue record for this book is available from the British Library

Library of Congress Cataloging in Publication Data
A catalog record for this book has been requested

ISBN: 978-1-138-12519-3 (hbk)
ISBN: 978-1-138-12523-0 (pbk)
ISBN: 978-0-203-73278-6 (ebk)

Typeset in Bembo
by diacriTech, Chennai

In memory of my beloved son, David Rosefielde

CONTENTS

FIGURES

TABLES

PREFACE

This year marks the 100th anniversary of the Bolshevik Revolution, the pivotal event that paved the way for the establishment of communism in China. It provides a fitting occasion for assessing an aspect of the Soviet communist legacy: China's communist experience and prospects. This volume probes China's communist dream, chronicles its evolution, investigates the properties of Xi Jinping's contemporary market communism, and evaluates future possibilities from a rigorous inclusive economic perspective. The Chinese communist experience has been largely a story of two rival visions of the true path to Golden Communism – Mao Zedong's revolutionary Red Communist (Command Communism) approach and Xi Jinping's technocratic White Communist (Market Communism) option. This dichotomy is the heart of our investigation, but it is incomplete because it conceals the larger perspective. China's market communist leaders do not have to choose between Red and White. There is a wide variety of Pink Communist and Liberal Democratic alternatives. The most attractive are surveyed to gauge China's best path forward.

ACKNOWLEDGEMENTS

This volume extends Abram Bergson's pioneering contributions to neoclassical welfare and socialist economic theory to the analysis of Chinese communism. Bergson was Professor Rosefielde's thesis advisor and mentor. Alex Nove, Sir Lionel Robins and Leonard Shapiro also were seminal influences. Quinn Mills, Chenyi Yu, Wenting Ma, Yiyi Liu, Zhikai Wang, Christine Tsai, Ehtisham Ahmad, Hasanat Syed, Yue Lai, Yuhan Wang, Diana Song and Siyu Zhao provided useful insights. Yunjuan Liu compiled the bibliography. Edwin Song prepared the graphs of Chapter 6. Susan Rosefielde, Yong Ling Lam and Samantha Phua gave essential encouragement. Professor Leightner acknowledges the help of Rebecca Smith and Sandra Leightner in finding news articles on China and the assistance of Xi Jin in finding information written in Chinese on Chinese laws. We express our sincere appreciation to all for their generous assistance.

INTRODUCTION

Xi Jinping (General Secretary of the Communist Party of China, the President of the People's Republic of China, and the Chairman of the Central Military Commission) faces a complex dilemma. He can try to improve China's technocratic market communism ("White Communism"),[1] or push forward (backward) to something better. He has chosen to advance by shifting the focus of China's development strategy from export- to import-substitution-led economic growth. He may succeed in achieving this limited objective, but the approach is too narrow. China's well-being does not depend on material progress alone. The right path ahead should enhance inclusive life quality (well-being).

Followers of Mao Zedong grasp this and urge a return to revolutionary "Red Communism." They consider the issue of export- versus import-substitution-led development extraneous. Mao's disciples want a more radical solution: a return to a pro-egalitarian command economy.

Xi and Mao both assume that communist ideals are internally consistent (universal harmonious actualization of every individual's full human potential in a freehold property-less world with non-coercive government), and are "scientifically" achievable. They both reject democracy and place their trust in the Communist Party of China (CPC), which claims to represent the people's will, but may not do so. China's revolutionary Red Communism in Mao's eyes and technocratic White Communism in Xi's view are not utopian, and pose no dystopian risk. This is why the CPC clings to the Communist Dream, steadfastly refusing to share political power or contemplate non-communist alternatives.

The internal debate which takes the CPC's and communism's superiority on faith revolves around a long-standing dispute over the comparative merit of political and economic regimes ruled by CPC "experts" (Deng Xiaoping school) or "reds" (Mao Zedong school). It avoids discussing blended options and excludes the possibility of democratic free enterprise or a host of other non-communist alternatives including Europe's social democracy, Confucian market systems, Japan's communalism, Piketty-type social justice regimes,[2] Trump's populism,[3] or even Tao Yuanming's utopian *Peach Blossom Spring*.

This treatise probes China's communist possibilities from the perspective of the "Great Debate" over ideal social systems,[4] with special attention paid to microeconomic production, distribution and transfer efficiency. Details about Mao's and Xi's policies are provided in endnotes.

Our investigation of China's communist possibilities begins with a complete description and analysis of China's contested communist systemic options, and then considers the merits of three non-communist alternatives: Liberal Democracy, globalism, and Asia's Confucian ideal. This is a "rational choice" approach.[5] The exercise suggests that even though the Chinese people may fare well enough under Red and White Communism, wise rulers in Beijing should not dismiss other candidates. Prudence demands an open-minded assessment of how mainlanders should lay their bets. This judgment holds regardless of the merit of specific policies and development strategies like Xi Jinping's "One Belt, One Road" scheme.

Although we believe that compassionate Liberal Democracy is China's best option, we refrain from advocating a best solution or prophesizing, leaving it to readers themselves to judge the Middle Kingdom's best path forward. As is widely understood, leaders do not always choose wisely.[6] It is unlikely that the Communist Party of China will carefully weigh all its systems options in deciding China's best rational choice.[7] Outcomes may well be path-dependent.[8] The virtue of the rational choice approach is that it clarifies possibilities, but this does not assure that reason will prevail.

PART I
Red Communism

1
POLITICS IN COMMAND

The Communist Party of China (CPC), founded July 1, 1921 by Chen Duxiu and Li Dazhao, seized control over the Middle Kingdom under the leadership of Chairman Mao Zedong on October 1, 1949.[9] Chen, Li and Mao were Marxists of diverse persuasions. Their notions of communist utopia and tactics differed, but all agreed on fundamentals. The task of the Chinese Communist Party was to eradicate capitalist political and economic rule, install a worker-peasant state, criminalize private property, the market and entrepreneurship, and establish an exploitation-free, harmonious, egalitarian order. The dictatorship of the proletariat (and peasants) was seen as a sine qua non to thwart counter-revolution and foster rapid industrialization during a "socialist" transition period, but all agreed that in the fullness of time the Communist Party would turn over the reins of government to self-regulating co-operators.

Chen's, Li's and Mao's notions of communism's future were visionary. They neither understood nor concerned themselves about technical economic feasibility. However, this was of little moment. All believed that communist rule meant revolutionary "politics in command" during the transition period.[10] The CPC's task was and is to fortify communist power and advance the communist cause as its leaders perceive it and necessity dictates without fretting about economic efficiency.[11]

Chinese leaders have interpreted this mandate in two broad ways. They embraced the Stalinist notion of command economy under Mao Zedong from 1950–1976 (with an anarcho-communist interlude during the Cultural Revolution),[12] and managed markets thereafter. Today both schools assume that the Communist Party will someday fully realize Karl Marx's communist vision elaborated in his *Economic and Philosophical manuscripts of 1844* and *The Communist Manifesto*,[13] and should this prove impossible, they intend to satisfice by striking the right balance.

The difference between the Maoist "red" and Xi Jinping's authoritarian "expert" model is simple. Mao's Red Communism proscribes private property, business and entrepreneurship, supplying society instead through requisitioning and rationing (under the Party's guidance or direct worker/peasant action), and enlists revolutionary spirit to combat bureaucratic abuses and promote communist egalitarianism.

Xi Jinping's technocratic regulated White Communist market system retains aspects of the command principle including state freehold ownership and planning, but supplements it with leasehold property and regulated private enterprise. Xi's market communism puts "experts" in charge and rejects "red" anarcho-communist zealotry. The dichotomy, in a nutshell, is "revolutionary" planning versus regulated market communism.

In Mao's world managers, workers and peasants are assigned tasks by the Communist Party or by the communist invisible hand in anarcho-communist moments. Comrades work for state fixed wages, or spontaneously cooperate. The Party commandeers, rations, distributes and sells goods to the people at state set prices. Anyone who does not work is a parasite, an offense punishable by forced labor in *laogai* (concentration camp).[14] Profits and rents belong to the state (people) and together with taxes fund public programs. The people are supplied with basic housing, transportation, energy, medical and educational services. The distribution of income is egalitarian because there are no private asset holders and managers receive neither profits nor rents. Mutual support further enhances social justice. Money and credit are not available for speculative purposes, eliminating financial crises. Resources are mobilized to spur technological progress and rapid economic development. Mao's command economy operated at full throttle, oscillating only with the winds of enthusiasm and labor effort. State wage and price-fixing kept inflation in check.[15]

Mao's command model was a macroeconomic dream come true. It provided overfull employment, price stability, business cycle-free production and rapid economic growth. Its primary drawbacks were labor coercion, consumer goods shortages (rationing) and shoddy merchandise. Workers and peasants were compelled to obey the Party and accept their lot. They could not acquire the goods they desired because it was illegal for consumers to negotiate with state suppliers. The system was a Spartan economy of shortage where everyone only received the basics because the lion's share of public expenditures was devoted to investment, defense and public goods. The supply of consumer goods gradually increased over time, but this meant little to people compelled to make do with things they did not want.

Citizens had limited opportunity to save and accumulate. They did not have to insure their property because they had none. They did not have to fret about foreign travel, transferring assets abroad, democratic action, civil rights or religion because everything not explicitly authorized by the Communist Party was forbidden.

This was a devil's bargain. Mao's communism provided macroeconomic robustness in exchange for compulsory labor, forced substitution and civil disempowerment. It gratified those who preferred a bare-boned egalitarian existence (pauper communism), and was an anathema to hedonists. The system was predicable because it could not be reformed from below. The Party repressed private initiative and civic action. If the Communist Party leaders were content with their devil's bargain, the people had to grin and bear it, barring a counter-revolution.

The counter-revolution happened. It came from within the Communist Party, gathering momentum after Mao Zedong died September 9, 1976. It was organized to overthrow aspects of the command paradigm and anarcho-communist zealotry in favor of economic power sharing between the Party and a new breed of leasehold entrepreneurs. Deng Xiaoping led the charge. He permitted Party and non-Party members to lease state assets and produce for domestic and foreign markets on a for-profit basis. International investors were encouraged to establish production facilities in special economic zones on the mainland. Deng allowed private, jointly owned and state companies to issue bonds and equity shares (for leasehold businesses) on domestic and foreign stock exchanges. The Renminbi (RMB) gradually became convertible. The Party provided financial support for speculative activities, and allowed prices and wages to be competitively negotiated.

This devolution of economic authority from the Communist Party to for-profit producers eliminated Mao's economy of shortage. Deng's new deal sacrificed macroeconomic robustness to preserve the Party's political monopoly, and achieve higher consumer satisfaction, substantial economic freedom, some civic liberalization and inequality. Xi Jinping's market communism today no longer sneers at economic efficiency and has zero tolerance for Red Guard militancy. It permits economic rewards to reflect marginal value added and has curbed forced substitution. The cost of this liberalization has been involuntary unemployment, inegalitarianism, social injustice, inflation, financial speculation, excessive debt and the increasing danger of financial crises.[16]

The leadership seems broadly satisfied with the new arrangements. This has led many to infer that China has abandoned communism for capitalism, but the judgment is superficial. The Communist Party remains at the helm. It directly controls the economy's commanding heights (the largest companies, including the military–industrial complex) and the supply of public goods. It is the freehold owner of the nation's land and entire productive capital stock, including property nominally classified as private. It has immense powers of taxation. It issues executive orders, mandates, rules and regulations at will, and rejects laissez-faire. The Communist Party acts as the economy's master puppeteer using all the instruments at its disposal including internal Party command to compel the economy to do its bidding, and can legally rescind leases and re-appropriate the nation's assets at its discretion. Consumers are only partially sovereign at the Party's sufferance, and the leadership appears to have no intention of sharing political power with rivals or building a democratic regime with full civil liberties under the rule of law.

Market communism despite these reservations is better for citizens who abhorred the excesses of the Cultural Revolution, but is a dubious bargain for egalitarians, Red Guardians and those who prize social solidarity. Xi Jinping and the Communist Party majority are under pressure to strike a better balance.

GDP growth has been decelerating and the threat of a major financial crisis is mounting. Mao's supporters are calling for accommodation, while others are pressing the case for democracy.[17]

What should be done? Should the Chinese Communist Party change course by paring or further empowering the market? Should it enhance anarcho-communism? Should it abandon or strengthen its dictatorship of the workers and peasants? People hold strong and opposing opinions on these matters based on their ethical, ideological, political, social, cultural and religious attitudes that allow them to disregard fundamentals. This puts the cart before the horse, caricaturing the Red Communist–White Communist split as a struggle between have nots and haves. The deeper issue is whether Marx's communism is attainable either as an ideal or acceptable approximation, and if so, whether communism is positively, normatively and ethically best.

Nobel Prizes have been awarded for mathematically proving the "existence" of a competitive market general equilibrium (Pareto optimality) covering production, distribution and transfers.[18] The proof shows how suppliers can optimally satisfy consumer's demands. A similar proof has been devised for the perfectly planned analogue of perfect competition given planners' preferences.[19] The correspondence is called the duality theorem, and provides substance to Chinese claims that planning theoretically is as good as competition. Moreover, mixed models combining markets and plans are easily constructed. This provides comfort for supporters of both Mao's command planning and Xi's market communism, but only supposing that planners know exactly what each and every individual wants (including transfers). This is the rub. Advocates of command planning, Cultural Revolution and market communism cannot construct a complete existence theorem that shows how the Communist Party and Red Guards know what individuals want (including transfers).[20] No Marxist has done so, and until such existence proofs are devised any debate between Maoists and Xi's supporters is shadow boxing. Neither approach can provide fully efficient production, distribution and transfers or fulfill arcane promises about full abundance (all goods are free), the abolition of exploitation of man by man, harmony and the full actualization of each individual's human potential. These goals are social romanticism.[21] There is no path to the promised land, even if Communist Party members were competent, well-intended and wise. Marx's and Stalin's meta-historical materialist dialectics don't save the day.[22]

This means that the comparative merit of Maoism and Xi-ism depends on the performance characteristics (positive economics) of Red Communism and White Communism in a bounded rational universe,[23] social justice and other normative considerations (ethics). Communist ideals, except insofar as they bear on social justice and ethics, are irrelevant and should not cloud normative judgments. What counts are the comparative levels of well-being that Mao's and Xi's systems provide, judged by wise and compassionate observers.

2

MAO ZEDONG

Mao Zedong's Red Army defeated the Kuomintang, conquered the mainland and established a one-party regime. Mao, the "Great Helmsman," was a military veteran and hardened partisan.[24] He became Chairman of the Communist Party in 1935, and was conversant with communist ideological politics. Stalin was his political mentor.[25] This background shaped Mao's perception of the main direction for constructing communist power in China. It impelled him to ruthlessly suppress the forces of counter-revolution[26] and follow the path pioneered by Stalin for building command communism, with some accommodation for local circumstances and many casualties.[27] Despite successes,[28] Mao understood that full Marxist utopian communism could not be gestated overnight. Tactical concessions were essential, but he believed that if the Party stayed the course, China would eventually reach the promised land.

The Great Helmsman's preference for Stalin's command model also was the path of least resistance. Soviet and Chinese communists shared the same ideological goals. The USSR despite great adversities rapidly industrialized after 1928, decisively defeated Hitler's armies and developed atomic and thermonuclear weapons. Perhaps other communist models including anarcho-communism (Cultural Revolutionary "redness") might have been better,[29] but there was little reason in 1950 to resist Stalin's bandwagon.[30]

Command economy

Mao from the outset chose to adopt Stalin's command economic framework with its complex "top-down" planning and "bottom-up" self-regulating mechanisms. The framework rested on three principles: the criminalization of private property (state freehold ownership of the means of production), the criminalization of markets (state requisitioning and rationing), and the criminalization of entrepreneurship (strict subordination of enterprise managers to Communist Party control).

Karl Marx contended that private ownership of productive assets allowed capitalists to misappropriate worker "surplus value," a problem that Stalin and Mao believed could be eradicated by nationalizing the means of production. Similarly, Marx recognized that market power (oligopoly and monopoly) enabled ruthless individuals to exploit the masses. The antidote here was to substitute state actors for private businesspersons. State-owned enterprises and distributive organizations (wholesale and retail) would be ordered to adhere strictly to government plans (requisitioning and rationing). Production would reflect social need, and distribution would be guided by the principles of communist justice.

Stalin and Mao also understood that state-appointed factory directors might violate communist duty by disregarding commands and acting entrepreneurially on their own behalf. China's Communist Party precluded the danger by requiring appointees to obey, imposing severe penalties for disobedience.

The criminalization of private property, markets and entrepreneurship stewarded by a wise Communist Party from Mao's perspective on the morrow of the revolution appeared to require a top-down system of state economic control. A self-regulating anarcho-communist system as Marx original envisioned was still thought to be best in the long run, after the state withered away, but was considered impractical in the first phase of socialist construction. The watchwords for top-down state economic control were plan and compliance. The Communist Party planned and supervised. Subordinates obeyed. Figure 2.1 illustrates the Soviet command concept for industrial production.

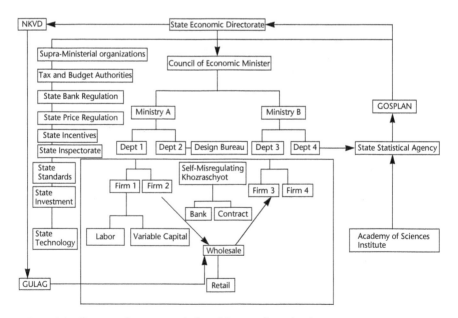

FIGURE 2.1 Command economy: industrial control mechanism.

The organization diagram is divided into three columns. Responsibility for planning is vested in scientific institutions, the State Statistical Agency (Goskomstat) and the State Planning Agency (Gosplan) displayed on the far right. Production, wholesaling and retailing are represented in the center column by firms and distributive channels, hierarchically supervised by the State Economic Directorate, the Council of Economic Ministers, industrial ministries and their subdivisions (main departments or glavks).

Command planning in this scheme is simplicity itself. Gosplan formulates aggregate plan assignments, approved by the General Secretary of the Communist Party, which are distributed down the supervisory command chain in the central column from the State Economic Directorate to ministries, departments and ultimately enterprise "Red directors" (obedient communist managers) who execute microplan assignments. There are no negotiations and no markets. Planners "scientifically" plan, and Red directors fulfill their assignments assuring consumer satisfaction. The system is top down with no self-regulating aspects.

This is the ideal. However, it was unattainable because central authorities had incomplete information and inadequate computational abilities. They had no knowledge of enterprise production functions, worker utility functions and consumer preferences, and lacked technical skills to achieve computopia.[31] This compelled the systems directors to use shortcuts that enabled them to plan broad aggregates (composite goods),[32] but delegated particulars to a host of regulators including Red directors.

Top-down planning occurred. Red directors were legally obliged to comply, but frequently could not do so because assignments were infeasible. Ministers, departments, party officials, military authorities and judicial institutions therefore were required to intervene and consult with red directors to salvage the situation. The process can be viewed as muddling through. It enabled the systems directors to control the broad contours of resource allocation and production through forced substitution, but not the fine print. Resources were not, and could not be put to best economic use.[33] Results were barely adequate from the consumer's perspective.

Stalin recognized as early as 1927 that top-down planning's limitations could be softened by supplementing plan assignments with a bottom-up self-regulating mechanism. Red directors were instructed to formulate their own incentive guided enterprise production plans [tekhpromfinplan (technical industrial financial plans)] that encouraged them to satisfice under constraint whenever plan assignments were infeasible or ill advised.[34] Engineering methods (eventually including linear and convex programming) were employed to calculate multi-input, multiproduct plans that maximized Red director bonuses.[35] Managerial rewards were variously tied to the physical volume of output, revenues and profit. Each incentive scheme had some merit, and in the case of profit encouraged Red directors to simulate the optimization protocol of competitive capitalist firms.

Chinese bottom-up bonus incentivized enterprise production made Mao's command economy self-regulating, even if plans were disobeyed, buttressed by a policy of guaranteed state purchase. Enterprise bank accounts were automatically credited when goods were collected at the factory door by the state's wholesale network. Red directors never needed to hedge production against the danger of weak consumer demand. They faced an infinitely elastic demand curve and produced near the simulated profit maximizing point (Figure 6.8).[36] In practice, this meant that Red directors automatically overproduced and overemployed workers because the State Price Committee deliberately added a large profit margin to state fixed prices above what would have been competitive equilibrium. This made Mao's command economy macro-economically effective and robust on a bottom-up basis. The mechanism, illustrated in Figure 2.1 by the box enclosing enterprises, factors of production, wholesaling, retailing, bank credit/debiting and contracts, was called "self-financing" (khozraschyot). The term conveys the notion that enterprises functioned independently, outside state budgetary control, but also has the broader implication of a non-competitive, non-negotiated, self-regulating bonus-seeking mechanism supported by assured state purchase.

Mao's command economy could have operated solely on a bottom-up basis. Red directors could have acted according to rule rather than assignment, misguided by "false" state fixed Marxist labor value-added fiat prices and arbitrary bonus incentives. The Communist Party, however, took a hands-on approach. It compelled Red directors to adjust their production programs to accommodate wishes expressed in top-down assignments and the demands of ministers, departments, party officials, military authorities, the secret police and judicial institutions.

Mao's command economy thus was a dual control top-down and bottom-up mechanism managed with political intervention. It was neither optimal, nor good. It was a weak satisficing regime that worked well enough from Mao's perspective by guaranteeing overproduction, overfull employment and economic growth driven by peasant migration to industry, new capital formation and technological progress.

The same basic principles held in agriculture. Mao sought to eradicate peasant exploitation by criminalizing large-scale private land ownership and agrarian markets.

Estates were collectivized and then communalized, and peasants were commanded by top-down plans. Collective and communal plans, like state industrial plans, were infeasible or undesirable for a multitude of reasons, and had to be supplemented by bottom-up peasant initiative. Conflicts between top-down plans and bottom-up initiatives were resolved ad hoc through political intervention.

Communist Party command over agriculture occurred in stages. First, land ownership was transferred from landlords to landless peasants under the Agrarian Reform Law of 1950 ("speak bitterness campaign"), and peasants were encouraged to cooperate in mutual aid teams. Second, starting in 1953, Mao adopted a radical collectivization program based on the Soviet model with intrusive Party agricultural control from above.[37] China's farmland was amalgamated into 25,000 mega communes, each with about 5,000 families, organized into "brigades" of about 200 families. The government made all decisions – farming methods, sale of crops, prices. Third, Mao forced peasants to combine industry with farming during the

"Great Leap Forward" in 1959–61, while at the same time President Liu Shaoqi allowed the peasants to own their own private plots, permitted bonuses and reduced the size of communes.[38]

The Great Helmsman's preference for a dual control top-down and bottom-up command industrial and agrarian economy was widely shared by Communist Party veterans, workers and peasants inspired by revolutionary idealism, proud that China had ended a "century of humiliation."[39] Affluence and consumer sovereignty were subsidiary, and shortages and forced substitution did not perturb China's leaders. Party activists, workers and peasants in the Mao era were revolutionary romantics. They desired an altruistic communitarian society founded on the principles of liberation, equality and public service captained by China's Communist Party. The Great Helmsman's command economy was adequate for their purposes as long as "experts" did not substitute an anti-"red" agenda. This danger was omnipresent.[40] Technocratic party officials held immense power both in the top-down and bottom-up spheres. They gradually came to feel that they deserved privileges and salaries commensurate with their superior social contribution.[41] Their attitude irked Red revolutionary idealists.

Mao appeared double-minded on the issue. He wanted to have his cake and eat it. The Great Helmsman desired better economic performance, but also favored an egalitarian order that permitted the concentration of political power in his own hands. He gradually came to the conclusion that anarcho-communist methods were needed to purge the command system, that top-down, bottom-up command should be abandoned.

Mao launched the Cultural Revolution in 1966 to reinvigorate China's redness.[42] It substituted "Red Guard" zealotry for Party technical supervision. Many viewed it as Chinese communism's defining moment. The Cultural Revolution was interpreted at home and abroad as anti-command, self-guiding communism from below liberated from technocratic state administration,[43] and has become an essential aspect of what contemporaries mean by Maoism. For most Maoists today, command is not enough. The alternative to Xi Jinping's market communism for them is not a technocratic expert-managed command economy. Rationing and requisition in their view must be consonant with and inspired by revolutionary, self-regulating economic action from below.[44] This is an opaque guideline,[45] but good enough to justify militant action – the Great Cultural Revolution.[46]

Mao's Red Guards and three-in-one committees did not abolish top-down or bottom-up planning.[47] They only weakened the influence of top-down planning and replaced fixed-price enterprise bonus maximizing with revolutionary zeal. Red Guards determined the right revolutionary thing to do as they perceived it, paying no heed to profit maximizing (and hence opportunity costs). They ignored efficiency, and refused to choose technology rationally.

Bottom-up planning continued, but was transformed. The system became Red Guard sovereign. Workers and peasants were employed, goods produced and distributed. Technologies were adopted and new investments made on the basis of revolutionary dogma, and weak top-down and regulatory guidance. This meant that outcomes could not be Party sovereign, or utopian ideal. They were satisficing results, given Red Guard preferences.

The Cultural Revolution did not reject Mao's macroeconomic goals. Red Guards sought to achieve full capacity utilization, full employment, stability and growth, but they substituted new revolutionary methods. Labor participatory management, replaced expert management stressing its egalitarian agenda.

Some comrades were enthralled by Red Guard anarcho-communism; others despised it. Clearly, the approach was ham-handed and could have been improved.[48] For example, Mao could have commanded the Red Guards and three-in-one committees to compute optimal enterprise micro-plans with expert assistance,[49] and could have taken externalities into consideration when assessing the public good.[50] These refinements would have integrate rational choice theory with redness without compromising revolutionary anarcho-communist sovereignty, and provided hope for those who continue to believe that Red Communism is best.[51]

Storming paradise

Mao's command model was designed to storm paradise. It was a revolutionary romantic frontal assault, insensitive to collateral damage. The strategy called for mobilizing labor, capital and natural resources to accelerate economic growth and development on an egalitarian basis for the community's benefit uncontaminated by privilege and rank. Utopian Marxist communism also promised full abundance, consumer satiation, complete actualization of human potential, harmony and the eradication of exploitation of man by man, but this could not be accomplished in the first stage of socialist construction. Maoists were reconciled to accepting half-a-loaf on the express train to socialism's second stage where individual demand would determine egalitarian supply and comrades would freely substitute leisure for labor.

China's top-down, bottom-up command planning regime was a modest success judged from the criteria Maoists set for themselves in the turnpike stage of socialist development (see Table 2.1), where everyone was expected to accept brute-forced substitution, labor mobilization and 35 million excess deaths as the price for tomorrow's utopia.[52]

The Cultural Revolution revealed that Reds and experts profoundly disagreed about the social merit of Mao's accomplishment and the benefits of staying the course, even though neither seemed perturbed by the carnage. Reds wanted more than an iron rice bowl[53] while awaiting the promised land, and experts wanted better lives for themselves. Others grudgingly were prepared to soldier on, despite growing impatience after wandering more than a quarter century in the desert of command planning. They wanted better social relations and higher levels of individual consumer satisfaction. The second stage of communist construction could not be achieved with the top-down, bottom-up command paradigm. Something would have to give. Reds would have to show that expert-free, self-regulating worker-managed communism was best, or experts would have to find a way of decriminalizing private property, markets and entrepreneurship without falling prey to capitalism's perils.

The experts prevailed. Mao's dual top-down and bottom-up command planning regime survived his death in 1976 for another two decades but gradually was replaced by market communism. Expert management was restored and Red Guard sentiment waned, but more importantly, the Communist Party leadership gradually lost faith in Mao's dual control top-down, bottom-up command model. It slowly came to the conclusion that Marx and Mao were wrong; that the good communist life couldn't be achieved if private property (leasehold), markets and entrepreneurship remained criminalized. Some kind of accommodation was essential if China desired prosperity and a leading role as a great power on the world stage.

This epiphany was a major turning point in Chinese Communist history. It allowed the Party to switch horses, ditching command for a mixed communist economy, but left three key issues unresolved: (1) Do the material benefits of market communism outweigh losses caused by inequality, despotism and macroeconomic dysfunction? (2) Can the contemporary market communist model be improved? (3) Are there superior third ways?

TABLE 2.1 Communist superindustrialization surges (Maddison's GDP series, thousand 1990 international Geary-Khamis dollars)

Period	Year	USSR	China	Cambodia
Holodomor	1931	275.2		
	1932	254.4		
	1933	264.9		
	1934	290.9		
Great Terror	1935	334.8		
	1936	361.3		
	1937	398.0		
	1938	405.2		
	1939	430.3		
	1940	420.1		
Great Leap Forward	1959		464.0	
	1960		448.7	
	1961		368.0	
	1962		368.0	

(*Continued*)

TABLE 2.1 Communist superindustrialization surges (Maddison's GDP series, thousand 1990 international Geary-Khamis dollars)(*Continued*)

Period	Year	USSR	China	Cambodia
	1963		403.7	
Cultural Revolution	1966		553.7	
	1967		537.0	
	1968		525.2	
	1969		574.7	
Year Zero	1974			5.0
	1975			4.3
	1976			4.7
	1977			5.0
	1978			5.5
	1979			5.6

Source: Angus Maddison, The World Economy: Historical Statistics, OECD: Geneva, 2003, Table 3b, p. 98; Table 5b, pp. 174, 178.

PART II

White Communism

3
DENG XIAOPING

Markets

Communism has no precise definition. The concept has been around for at least 2400 years,[54] with a root meaning of communitarian egalitarian sharing. Commune members work for the common good, and distain economic and social inequality, except in cases where individuals have special legitimate needs (supplementary assistance to the handicapped). Competitive markets are superfluous under communism because communards are not motivated by profit and utility-seeking at the expense of fellow members. Moreover, most communists feel that markets and sharing are incompatible. Markets are driven by people's urge for competitive self-advancement and acquisitiveness. Economic rivals place personal interest ahead of community need.

Communism is suited to a rustic environment adorned by the joys of friendship and sharing, a sentiment echoed in Tao Yuanming's *Peach Blossom Spring* narrative written during the Six Dynasties (220–589 AD).[55] Complex versions of the good communist life promised in Marx's *Economic and Philosophical Manuscripts of 1844* also may be possible, but more difficult to achieve because Marx assumes that communards have diverse tastes, aptitudes and inclinations that should be fully satisfied. In complex societies individuals aren't able to directly determine other people's needs. They cannot intuit best technologies. Individuals cannot intuit the best use of resources, optimally produce or distribute.

This confronts communists with a predicament. They can settle for the simple life enriched by art, poetry, music, wine and warm communality practiced since Tao Yuanming's time by some Chinese literati,[56] or grapple with the contradictions entailed by prosperity-seeking for a community where acquaintances have diverse needs.[57] Mao's command model attempted to solve the dilemma through rapid economic growth and development, but planning did not suffice,[58] setting the stage for a fresh approach. Deng Xiaoping stepped into the breach.[59] He argued that markets could be engineered to serve the people through trial and error experimentation and set about testing the conjecture by "crossing rivers touching stones one at a time."[60]

Deng's goal was not transforming Mao's command communism into laissez-faire market capitalism.[61] He envisioned a mixed economy that used managed markets to mitigate some of planning's and anarcho-communism's technical shortcomings.[62] This approach had been rejected during the first stage of communist construction when the top priority was establishing Party rule, but later became attractive as a device for tapping underutilized aspects of China's economic potential.[63] Market communism in Deng's view was a means to the end, not the end in itself. He believed that the benefits of managed markets would outweigh the costs during the second stage of communist construction,[64] and they might even serve a positive role under full communism.[65]

Crossing rivers one stone at a time

The command planning diagram (Figure 2.1) presented in Chapter 2 provides insight into Deng's thinking. Mao's entire top-down, bottom-up control mechanism is preserved in the White Communist model, with four important modifications. First, the state is no longer sole owner of the means of production. Leasehold ownership, both state and private, coexist instead allowing some people to accumulate wealth from their non-labor assets. Second, central plans which were often ignored under Red Communism are no longer formally compulsory. White Communism accepts that central plans are mostly indicative.[66] Indicative central plans guide managers instead of commanding them. Third, Red directors reincarnated as Red managers are free to act as CEOs without Maoist restrictions.[67] Red managers can lease and competitively operate their firms choosing least cost vendors and the most avid buyers. They can negotiate wages and prices, select technologies, import and export, borrow and lend, float bonds and stock shares, franchise, merge and acquire. They are entitled to dividends on their leasehold ownership stakes, and may receive owner-approved performance bonuses.[68] Fourth, leasehold private entrepreneurship is decriminalized. Red directors under Deng's White Communism are permitted to lease state property and use it to start new businesses for their private benefit.

From a diagrammatic perspective (Figure 2.1), these changes mean that the directive chains of command in the central column and horizontal planning links among enterprises and state institutions (the State Bank and compulsory contracting) have been abolished and replaced by market competition. The system mimics competitive Western relations differing only in two aspects: (1) prohibitions on private freehold ownership, and (2) the Communist Party's role in shaping economic regulation and control through the columns on the far right and left. These special features preserve the Party's authority and make it "sovereign." China's Communist Party has the power to set the rules of economic conduct (its version of Locke's social contract)[69] and control the courts to promote communist ends, and can cancel leases at its discretion. It may encourage Pareto efficiency when this seems appropriate, but the Party mostly imposes forced substitution with indirect means. The market is not king. It is merely the Party's post-Maoist handmaiden.

Market Communism: first phase 1978–1989

Deng Xiaoping's strategy of "crossing rivers one stone at a time" unfolded in phases. The first phase, often called Gaige Kaifang ("reforms and openness"), lasted more than a decade from the defeat of the Gang of Four (Jiang Qing, Mao's last wife Jiang Qing, Wang Hongwen, Zhang Chunqiao and Yao Wenyuan) on October 6, 1976 (by Hua Guofeng, Wang Dongxing, Wu De and Chen Xilian) until shortly after the Tiananmen Square massacre, June 5, 1989. The goal was the gradual reversal of the three ideological pillars of the command economy: criminalization of private property, criminalization of private business and criminalization of entrepreneurship. This was Marxist-Stalinist heresy and had to be cautiously undertaken.

The Party granted citizens the right to lease property from the state on a fixed-term basis (as distinct from freehold proprietorship), engage in for-profit business and start new businesses, either privately or as state enterprise managers. Peasants and businesses (private and state) also were given the right to negotiate prices and wages (which required the abolition of state price and wage fixing) and permitted to borrow funds from the state bank. They were regulated instead of controlled and freed from the obligation to obey plan directives.

These new business rights emulated liberal free enterprise, but the regime remained illiberal because the Communist Party (CPC) fully intended to assume the role of master puppeteer, retaining its monopoly of state power, restrictions on civil liberties, the criminalization of freehold property, ownership of the economy's "commanding heights" (banking, financial holding companies, defense and foreign trade), insider state contracting and energetic market regulation. The Communist Party's strategy was to harness people's productive energies, including foreign investors, and permit increased consumer choice, while preserving its ultimate illiberal economic sovereignty by deftly using the regulatory and control instruments at its disposal to pull the people's strings. The Communist Party's concept of power remained top down (self-appointed authorities who control and regulate consumers), in contrast to democratic free enterprise, which is bottom up (consumers control private sector suppliers and elected government agents).

The years immediately after Mao Zedong's death (1976) until the start of Gaige Kaifang were inauspicious. It seemed initially that Hua's new post-coup d'etat regime would be conservative (reformist command planning), but Deng Xiaoping (whose power base was inside the Communist Party, rather than a state figurehead) succeeded in reversing the tide around 1978 by pressing the four modernizations (agriculture, industry, science and technology, and the military), without debating the relative importance of plans and markets. He praised the "household-responsibility system" (allowing peasant family households to operate their plots semi-independently), which made it possible for them to prosper by increasing productivity and selling above quota output in collective farm markets and household (cottage) industries, in 1980.[70] Soon the principle was applied nationwide, even though the practice had been considered counterrevolutionary when collective farmers in Xiaogang and Fengyang informally experimented with the technique in 1978. The scheme sometimes involved incentives without markets, sometimes with them.[71]

The household-responsibility system was quickly coupled with the "town and village enterprise" (TVE) movement, an effort to transform the separate profit-seeking activities of individual households into a coordinated agro-industrial communal business.[72] This hybrid institution further shifted communal management rights from central administrators to production brigades, and households, overseen by local officials. TVE member households did not own land and capital in perpetuity (freehold property);[73] nonetheless, they had informal leasing rights to operate assets and sell produce for a sufficient period to make profit-seeking reasonable. TVEs were flexible, and enjoyed considerable discretion in undertaking agro-industrial activities. The idea of integrating agriculture and industry (mostly handicrafts and light manufacturing) within a unitary institutional framework echoed the Great Leap Forward, when peasants were compelled to produce backyard steel, but Deng's version was more flexible allowing locally controlled TVEs to prosper. The TVE workforce quadrupled from 28 million to 135 million from 1978 to 1993, and contributed significantly to aggregate Chinese economic growth.[74] As time passed by many TVEs began operating de facto as private enterprises, despite their cooperative form,[75] and prospered in part due to the dearth of freehold property owning competitors,[76] and state financing.[77] These halcyon days lasted until the mid-1980s when communes and collectives were broken up or abandoned and their land divided among individual households into parcels as small as a fifth of an acre.[78] A half-acre of land per person was the typical allotment. Although peasants only acquired long-term, renewable leasing rights, as distinct from freehold ownership, individual households strenuously competed with TVEs for market share, weakening TVEs as a force in the countryside. Today, China's 600 million farmers are semi-independent,[79] even though they still raise crops on government land, and sell to state-owned grain companies, because they enjoy considerable operational freedom.

Deng did not confine his command modernization initiatives to domestic production. He pioneered joint ventures between foreign companies and Chinese state enterprises and following Hua's example promoted Special Economic Zones (SEZ),[80] the first in Shenzhen in 1980 and then in Zhuhai, Xiamen and Shantou (the "coastal strategy"). Deng also extended material incentives to large-scale industry, emulating Taiwan and South Korea. Nearly 22,000 joint ventures were launched in the SEZs (952 with American firms like Chrysler and Coca-Cola) in 1989. The bulk of the initial direct foreign investment came from overseas Chinese. SEZs developed slowly at first, but succeeded spectacularly in the 1990s.

Gaige Kaifang raised productivity and real income.[81] However, forced substitution exaggerated the magnitude of these gains. The state, not competitive markets, fixed prices circa 1979 precluding consumer sovereignty. Buyers could choose, but could not influence, the supplies and product characteristics. Consumers were compelled to purchase things they would have refused if prices had been competitive. Policymakers recognized the problem in the early 1980s, responding at first by setting multiple prices for the same goods to promote this or that objective, and then later allowed industrial enterprise managers to set their own prices,[82] with an eye toward expanding sales and bonuses. Only a small number of industrial product prices were market determined in early 1986, but this changed rapidly. By the early 1990s, the forces of supply and demand determined most industrial prices.[83] By the early 1990s, import tariffs were cut in half, starting a gradual process reducing all import barriers, and tax and subsidy policies were rationalized.

Many observers concluded that liberalization had placed China on the high road to free enterprise just prior to the Tiananmen Square massacre, but the judgment was premature,[84] because partial deregulation and Leninist New Economic Policy (NEP) style state market management are not the same things as consumer sovereign liberal free enterprise (see Chapter 6).[85] The post-revolutionary Communist Party pulling billions of marionette strings remained fully in command. It was economic sovereign, not consumers whose influence over supply was tightly circumscribed.

Communism often employed material incentives to motivate production in ways consistent with planners' choice.[86] Soviet workers during the 1930s received progressive piecework bonuses tied to the fulfillment and over-fulfillment of production quotas, together with privileged access to scarce consumer goods. Some products were subsidized. Collective farmers negotiated prices with private purchasers. The Party insisted that all these measures were compatible with socialism because they furthered government goals. Stalin's, Khrushchev's, Brezhnev's, Mao's and Deng's preferences determined ownership and user rights, aggregate economic structure, investment, supply characteristics, assortments, distribution and finance, not those of consumers and other final purchasers. Any economic system can employ material incentives, and permit negotiated transaction. Only those that allow consumer demand to govern supply are authentic consumer sovereign regimes. Otherwise, they are command, controlled, administrated, managed and/or regulated economic systems.[87]

Deng Xiaoping's regime before the 1990s was a communist command planning economy, administered, managed and partly regulated with material incentives, and a patchwork of local markets lacking secure business and entrepreneurial rights. The regime was anti-democratic, employed forced penal labor (laogai, laojiao), maintained the world's largest standing army and suppressed civil society. People had only limited rights to travel outside their locales, rationing persisted and families were restricted to having one child (1979 to 2016).[88] Deng Xiaoping's slogan "To get rich is glorious" may have reverberated with Confucians, but communist Chinese reality was Dickenseque. Economic liberalization was beneficial, but Chinese communism remained light years away from Marx's communist ideal. The Tiananmen events showed the depth of popular discontent.[89] Student grievances were diverse,[90] and did not amount to a clarion call to accelerate White Communism, but the Party ultimately concluded this was the wisest course.

Market Communisn: second phase 1992–2012

The second phase of Deng Xiaoping's march to market communism began in 1992, when he undertook his famous "Southern Tour" to Shenzhen. During the trip, Deng characterized China's emerging White Communist system as a "socialist market economy,"[91] and asserted that "If China does not practice socialism, does not carry on with 'reform and opening' and economic development, does not improve the people's standard of living, then no matter what direction we go, it will be a dead end." This clarion call to reinvigorate liberalization in the aftermath of the Communist Party's post-Tiananmen Square retrenchment succeeded.[92] Deng sidelined central planners like Chen Yun, and installed Zhu Rongji to oversee the next, more consumer-empowering wave of White Communization, pressing forward with market liberalization, mass urbanization and development.

Deng's team promptly transformed Red directors into managers of competitive state-owned enterprises (SOEs), and then ultimately into managers of private companies by expanding and codifying their powers in "The Regulations on Transforming the Management Mechanism of State-Owned Industrial Enterprises," issued July 1992. The document granted managers 14 control rights over (1) production, (2) pricing, (3) sales, (4) procurement, (5) foreign trade, (6) investment, (7) use of retained funds, (8) disposal of assets, (9) merger and acquisitions, (10) labor, (11) personnel management, (12) wages, (13) bonuses and (14) internal organization, and allowed for refusal to pay unauthorized charges by the government.[93]

These rules mimicked the rights of western firms, but had less force because managers were not protected by the rule of law (independent judiciary). The Communist Party at its discretion could violate its own administrative decrees. Still, the new rules meant that under favorable circumstances state-owned enterprises could supply other government entities and private consumers more efficiently.

The potential gains were obvious, but so too were the liabilities. The command principle might still supersede the market. Managers might prefer to remain inert accepting state procurement contracts and subsidies instead of competitively profit-seeking, and moral hazard might distort Deng's reforms. Instead of acting scrupulously on the state's behalf, managers might privatize state revenues and assets to themselves. This type of corrupt behavior is called adverse selection. Agents, who are supposed to serve the state, serve themselves instead at the people's expense.

However, Deng's Communist Party successors, Zhu Rongji,[94] Jiang Zemin[95] and Hu Jintao, were undaunted.[96] They solved the moral hazard problem by accommodating it. The CPC allowed managers, and others including the taizidang (sons and daughters of high party officials often derogatorily called princelings), to lease state assets, close unsuccessful state enterprises, merge and acquire leased companies, enter into foreign joint ventures at home and abroad, and become billionaires.[97]

It preserved Marxist principles by maintaining the state monopoly over freehold property and vigilant Party supervision.[98]

Zhu's, Jiang's and Hu's decision to construct a White Communist system that privileged insiders, and offered limited economic opportunity to everyone else, has been partly concealed behind a smokescreen of ambiguous corporate property rights. Chinese companies fall into two broad categories: private firms and state-owned enterprises (SOE). The distinction is subtle. "Privately owned" firms are leaseholds with majority private proprietorship. The state can be and is often a minority stake leaseholder in "privately owned companies." No Chinese private leasehold enjoys freehold property rights, and in this sense China's means of production remain state (people) owned. Freehold capitalism does not exist on the mainland.

SOEs are freehold state property. The state leases its freehold properties on a fixed tenure basis to CEOs who operate them for profit.[99] CEOs at their discretion are permitted to sell their company's leasehold to insiders (including themselves) and others, domestically and on foreign stock exchanges (often described as "listed companies"). Many speak loosely of this ownership and leasehold management scheme as capitalist because it operates for profit. The scheme does resemble franchising in the West (like McDonalds), but it is not the same thing. Leasehold property is voluntary in the West. It is compulsory in White Communist China.[100]

The state protects its freehold interest by retaining 51 percent of enterprise shares, and can hire and fire CEOs and other managerial personnel at its discretion. Shareholders consequently do not have derivative freehold property rights, and merely own entitlements to revenues generated during the life of the lease. Communist Party insiders determine the terms of these implicit leases and allow them to grant custodial rights to themselves, their families and friends. Thus, while SOE's are formerly state freehold property, they have become leasehold vehicles for enriching members of the Communist Party, subject to the regulatory supervision of the State-owned Assets Supervision and Administration Commission (SASAC).

The imprecise use of the term "state" further obscures the White Communist essence of China's market system. Many commentators assume that state refers to the central government in Beijing, but it also may apply to provincially and municipally owned enterprises depending on context.

There were more than 150,000 SOEs in 2012 before Xi assumed power, controlled by the central, provincial and municipal governments,[101] some operating in protected (closed) sectors including defense, but the numbers are shrinking gradually due to mergers and acquisitions. The trend holds for all categories of SOEs including Red Chips (CITC, COSCO, China Resources, Beijing Enterprise, etc.) traded abroad on the Hong Kong stock exchange. Red Chip SOEs can be considered China's "commanding heights."[102] There were 159 active mega-conglomerate SOEs of this type at the end of 2006, and 110 in 2016.[103]

This consolidation, together with the disappearance of Mao-era heavily industrial "dinosaurs," has led some to suppose that SOEs are vanishing, but this is myopic. Merged SOEs are thriving. SOEs control at least 40 percent of non-agriculture economic activity. They are profitable, and growing thanks to hidden subsidies,[104] but remain inefficient because they are obligated to satisfy the government's political objectives.[105] It is also important to remember that private firms are majority private share leaseholds. They too are state-owned firms, but just of another type.

Foreign joint ventures including Alcatel, Motorola and Volkswagen are subject to similar leasing restrictions, even though they act as freehold corporations outside of China. The SASAC has substantial influence over their operations. Its sway however is less for small state and collective entities controlled by local governments; private groups in the competitive sectors, increasingly acting like conglomerates; and small private and family collective commercial firms in the urban and rural service sectors.[106]

These developments together with parallel stock market and banking reforms have allowed SOEs to increase equity (shares) sales to outsiders, and banks to tighten credit discipline over profligate SOEs.[107] They also have facilitated market-driven reshuffles of corporate structure through mergers and acquisitions (M&A), neither initiated nor tightly controlled by the SASAC.

The greater good in this permissive communist variant no longer depends on protecting the people's assets from embezzlers, preventing the diversion of government revenues and insider rent-granting.[108] The primary concern of the Communist Party, through the SASAC and other instruments, is enriching privileged SOE insiders and their families and friends with contracts, incentives, regulations, credit access, mandates, subsidies, quotas and tariffs. This for many Maoists is a betrayal of the revolutionary Marxist (and Tao Yuanming) cause, and was Stalin's explicit justification for abolishing NEP. Deng may have intended to keep a lid on income inequality in the 1980s,[109] but his technocratic White Communist successors decided otherwise.[110]

The distinctive features of the second phase of China's anti-egalitarian market communism are modestly rising incomes for the common man and extravagantly wealthy privileged insiders. The Party has not impoverished the people.[111] It only has appropriated the lion's share of the spoils to itself by awarding insiders with privileged use of leased state assets, actively supporting favored SOEs with lucrative contracts, subsidies, etc., and pulling a billion marionette strings to assure their enrichment. Some call this market capitalism,[112] but it is unvarnished technocratic White Communism, the second stage of socialist construction before the arrival of the Golden Communist utopia.

Sources of success

The performance of White Communism during the second phase was excellent judged from the benchmarks of modernization, growth and development, despite the regime's anti-competitive inequities. Official statistics as is widely understood significantly exaggerate accomplishments, nonetheless, evidence from a multitude of sources confirms that China made substantial progress building a modern infrastructure, and an export-oriented industrial sector. China has become the "workshop of the world." Beijing was clogged with bicycles a quarter century ago; today automobiles congest the roads bumper to bumper, and the same scene is repeated in large provincial cities like Chengdu.

How was this possible in an anti-democratic White Communist system? In pondering the matter, it is worth recalling that the Soviet Union and Maoist China both claimed similar successes under command communism. Anti-competitiveness, authoritarianism and social injustice do not preclude rapid economic growth in some epochs. Stalin's and Mao's centrally planned regimes both invested heavily, gave citizens solid technical educations, incentivized effort and transferred technology from abroad. Their Red Communism did not produce things consumers wanted, but the official data never reflected the deficiency. Forced substitution compelled consumers to buy whatever they could find.

White Communism improved matters by making supply more responsive to private consumer on the Party's terms. The growth officially claimed reflected real improvements, better than the phantom accomplishments of Mao's Great Leap Forward, and allowed China to narrow the gap with Western living standards.

A key to this success was technology transfer. White Communism attracted more than a trillion dollars of foreign direct investment (FDI) to China's shores. This inflow of superior technology, knowhow and marketing skills worked miracles, and cost the Communist Party nothing. Foreign outsourcers, drawn by the lure of cheap resources and a disciplined work force, built turnkey facilities designed to international specifications, transferred technologies and manufactured branded products that enabled China to rapidly climb the value-added ladder, producing inexpensively at home and selling favorably abroad. Resources used to produce goods with Chinese characteristics in the domestic market fetched little, but the same resources redeployed to foreign outsourcers were immensely profitable. Technological diffusion leveraged these gains. Chinese engineers copied foreign technologies and spread them across the economy, increasing White Communism's growth momentum.[113]

Deng's, Zhu's, Jiang's and Hu's gambit worked. China succeeded in modernizing far faster and more effectively than it could have if the party had chosen to rely on domestic innovation, as the Maoist experience amply confirms. The decisive role played by outsourcing and technology transfer does not detract from China's advance, but it does affect the assessment of White Communism's prospects, because potential returns to technology transfer are rapidly depleting. China's growth began decelerating, and could soon asymptotically converge to the rate of international technology progress (a couple of percent per annum) in accordance with advanced economic theory.[114] This means that even if anti-competitive privilege granting does not hobble White Communism, China's economy cannot grow faster than a few percent per annum in the decade ahead.[115] Xi Jinping perceives the danger, but does not fully comprehend it. He still has not come to grips with the fact that if Beijing remains committed to White or Red Communism, China must redesign its economic mechanism to reconcile the conflicting claims of social justice and prosperity in an era of flagging economic growth.

4

XI JINPING

Xi Jinping is the General Secretary of the Communist Party of China, the President of the People's Republic of China, and the Chairman of the Central Military Commission. He came to power in November 2012 and holds the honorary title of "core leader",[116] previously accorded to Mao Zedong, Deng Xiaoping and Jiang Zemin, but not Hu Jintao. Xi is the voice of Communist China looking toward the third and final phase of communist construction. What does the record of his first four years in power reveal about the Communist Party's intentions? Does it suggest that China is ready to redesign Deng's market governance mechanism to reconcile the conflicting claims of egalitarianism and prosperity in an era of retarded economic growth? Does it indicate that the Party believes that it is still premature to implement Marx's Golden Communist Dream? Has Xi invented a White Communist Dream that surpasses Marx's own utopia? Is China's Communist Party in the throes of joining the globalist bandwagon, abandoning communism altogether in favor of a democratic Western-style socially just, government-managed market system with freehold private property?

Xi's Chinese Dream

Xi has a Chinese Dream. It is both a vision and an action plan for a brighter tomorrow.[117] Xi's goals are rapid socialist economic development, prosperity and national glory achieved through collective effort under the guidance of China's Communist Party.[118] Supporters characterize it as "the essence of socialism with Chinese characteristics."[119] The dream seeks to realize the "Two 100s": a "moderately well-off society" by 2021, and full national development by 2049, the 100th anniversary of the founding of the People's Republic.[120]

Xi could have added economic and social equality, a robust social safety net, entitlements, affirmative action, restorative justice, full civil liberties and democracy to his agenda, but chose not to do so. He has done nothing to redesign Deng's White Communist mechanism to reconcile the conflicting claims of egalitarianism and prosperity. Instead, he decided behind closed doors that economic and social egalitarianism are not immediate communist priorities. The Communist Party of China (CPC) seems to believe that social justice and full civil liberties are secondary aspects of communism indefinitely postponed.[121]

Staying Deng's course

Xi's prosperity and power-first White Communist agenda means that he intends to continue crossing Deng Xiaoping's rivers one stone at a time, a task easily accomplished because his predecessors already have done most of the heavy lifting.

They introduced leasehold ownership, labor mobility, managerial choice, entrepreneurship, stock markets, derivatives,[122] mergers and acquisitions, floating exchange rates, liberalized international trade and direct foreign investment. The only unfinished business is fine-tuning supply side market incentives, re-invigorating development, improving macroeconomic management and purging corruption.

Economic development is the strategy's heart and soul, founded on three themes: (1) import substitution, (2) domestic consumption and (3) "One Belt, One Road" (OBOR). The first two initiatives involve structural adjustment. Deng Xiaoping wagered on an export-driven development strategy that attracted abundant foreign investment to China's shores, turbo-charged technology transfer and bloated Beijing's foreign currency reserves. He achieved these goals by undervaluing the RMB, giving exporters hidden subsidies, encouraging foreign outsourcers and relying on robust international import demand. The environment that supported this strategy however soured in the wake of the 2008 global financial crisis, reducing export returns and increasing the attractiveness of import substitution. Hu responded appropriately. He took steps to facilitate domestic consumption like providing workers with more shopping time, appreciating the RMB exchange rate and reducing export subsidies. The resulting structural shift was economically warranted and desirable on multiple grounds, but did not fundamentally change the system beyond slowing the inflow of foreign currency reserves, shaving state savings and increasing the supply of domestic consumer goods. Economic growth was already raising living standards,[123] and the additional consumer gains from import substitution were modest.

Xi Jinping's OBOR project is another kettle of fish.[124] It provides a majestic framework to keep China humming. The Middle Kingdom's tried and true engine of development since the days of Qin Shi Huang Di (220–210 BC) has been public works construction.[125]

Xi wants to continue the tradition partly by diverting investment from China's over-developed East (coastal provinces) to the interior, and by extending its infrastructure across the globe to Central Asia, Southeast Asia, Pakistan and even Europe, co-funded with the newly created Asian Infrastructure Investment Bank (AIIB).[126] The scheme kills three birds with one stone. It provides the regime with a politically palatable justification for shifting investment funds from coastal power centers to the West, identifies desirable infrastructure growth nodes and enhances Beijing position as a superstar on the global stage. Critics dismiss the vision as Xi's folly,[127] and could be right, but from a systems perspective OBOR symbolizes the Deng–Xi White Communist concept of China's destiny. The hallmarks of Xi's China Dream are state power, magnificence and prosperity, not Liberal Democracy, or Red social justice.

It is important to appreciate that the Deng–Xi approach is narrowing the per capita income divide between the East and West, despite restraints on individual liberty and freehold property rights, and that China is succeeding in its drive to become a great military and technological power. The US Department of Defense's annual reports to Congress testify to these successes. Before 2016 DoD reports confidently asserted that Chinese living standards would cease converging toward the West's high frontier as the advantages of economic backwardness faded, that Beijing could not master advanced technologies and did not wish to build conventional and nuclear forces rivaling America's. The 2016 report suddenly is mute on all these articles of faith,[128] signaling that Deng–Xi White Communist modernization is transforming China into a bona fide superpower with profound systemic implications.[129]

The CPC's Deng–Xi faction now has potent ammunition for preserving the White Communist status quo without accommodating Red Communist rivals. China's post-Mao economic and military accomplishments allow insiders to continue enjoying the fruits of economic and social inequality, while claiming to be the people's revolutionary best friend, promising slowly improving living standards, a "sky blue life,"[130] and muscular national power. Nationalist glory has replaced the communist internationalism of the 1960s and 1970s. It is the regime's raison d'etre and guiding star, not Redness.

Xi has built on this accomplishment with mundane reforms that do not require thorough examination,[131] and by buttressing his claim to be the people's revolutionary best friend with a high profile anti-corruption campaign after the 18th National Congress of the Communist Party in November 2012. He cracked down on "tigers and flies,"[132] high-level officials and local civil servants alike, dismissing indicted officials for bribery and abuse of power. As of 2016, the campaign has "netted" over 120 high-ranking officials, including about a dozen senior military officers, several major executives of state-owned companies and five national leaders. More than 100,000 people have been indicted for corruption.[133] The campaign is notable in implicating both incumbent and former national-level leaders, including former Politburo Standing Committee (PSC) member Zhou Yongkang and former military leaders Xu Caihou and Guo Boxiong.

Xi's determination is impressive, and holds out a ray of hope that the CPC will purge White Communism's illiberal blemishes, that Golden Communism

(Marx's dream) is possible even though the Party remains riddled with corruption.[134] China's public applauds Xi's actions, but this does not settle the larger debate between revolutionary Red Communism and technocratic White Communism about the best way to achieve Golden Communism, or a Pink Communist compromise. What should be done? Should the CPC move toward Red, Pink or Golden Communism,[135] or something better?

PART III
The great debate

5

RED VERSUS WHITE

Scholars, politicians, visionaries and activists have been debating the nature, premises, feasibility and comparative merit of Marx's Golden Communism since 1844.[136] The Chinese version of the debate has focused on the Red Communist and White Communist quarrel over best path to human progress, presuming that CPC rule is better than a democratic liberal order.

Maoists reject the White Communist road because Reds believe that Marx was right: Golden Communism proscribes private property and markets, and the rich and powerful will never willingly transfer their assets and privileges to the people, or cease exploiting the masses.

White Communists reject Maoism because they believe experience has taught them that the full abundance promised in Marx's Dream necessitates leasehold private property and managed markets. White Communists contend that private property and markets are preconditions for Golden Communism's success.

The debate is irresolvable because Marx's Dream is paradoxical. Communists cannot achieve egalitarian harmony if they tolerate private property and markets that allows some to be wealthier and more powerful than others; and they cannot have prosperity and full abundance if they ban private property and markets![137] Catch-22.[138]

Pink Communism

There is no communist resolution to this dilemma, only a Pink Communist compromise. White dilutes red, and red colors white. Pink is the blend, but it is not golden.[139] If Maoists and Xi's disciples want to bury their hatchets and unite in a common cause to build a better communist future, they must abandon the chimera of Golden Communism and reach a consensus on how to combine market forces with social justice in a pragmatic communist society. This involves behavioral and ethical judgments about balancing democracy with party control, personal freedom with social justice, value-add-based pay with egalitarianism, and entitlement with equality. Just as in other societies, China must decide the specific powers of co-sovereign political rulers, social forces and individuals to achieve high states of national well-being.

Red Communists can relax objections to individual self-seeking in varying degrees, while urging White Communists to "serve the people." White Communists can place social duty above acquisitiveness and personal advancement in varying degrees, while urging Red Communists to accept some inequality. Reds and Whites together can dispense with the Communist Party's monopoly on political power, and legalize freehold property.

The proof of Pink Communist systems is in the pudding, not their Olympian promises. Results, not possibilities, are what matter. The historical record suggests that while White Communism is preferable to Mao's command and Cultural Revolutionary regimes from a material and libertarian perspective,[140] a shift toward Pink Communism should improve overall well-being. It should be possible to make China more materially and socially egalitarian in Xi Jinping's world through multiple channels, including tax transfers, without seriously impairing economic efficiency and growth.[141] It also should be possible to strengthen civil liberties, personal freedom, diversity, democracy and social justice by devolving greater authority to the people. Reds are convinced that the experiment is worth trying and are probably right. [142]

None of this of course means that Pink Communism is better than Liberal Democracy, globalism, Trump populism, Taiwanese Confucianism, Tao Yuanming's *Peach Blossom Spring,* or numerous other non-communist systems. We will return to this issue later.

6

LIBERAL VERSUS ILLIBERAL

The "Great Debate" over communism's comparative merit started shortly after the French Revolution. It gathered momentum after Karl Marx's publication of the *Communist Manifesto* in 1847, and dominated global politics after the Bolshevik Revolution in 1917 until the Soviet Union's demise in 1991. Russia's Communist Party lingers on, but from the early 1990s to the present, history's verdict from the West's perspective has been that communism failed the competitive test.[143] This judgment however is only valid for Soviet and North Korean command communism.[144] Chinese White Communism has more than held its own against the imperfectly competitive Liberal Democratic orders of the West since emerging full-fledged in the new millennium, and Pink Communist markets could do better.

The "Great Debate" about communism today for open-minded intellectuals therefore no longer hinges on the merit of planning versus the market; it now turns on whether Liberal Democracies of the classic Western type are better than Illiberal CPC-controlled White or Pink Communist systems. White and Pink Communists contend that their managed markets promote well-being the best.

The claim is threefold. First, White and Pink Communists assert that the CPC knows and honors its duty. Second, they insist that communist duty fosters effort better than liberal indulgence. Third, they contend that leasehold markets are better than freehold systems.[145]

The evaluation of these claims requires an appreciation of the challenges of CPC market management, the virtues of freehold property and a thorough understanding of competitive Liberal Democratic market principles. This chapter elaborates the fundamentals and draws a few large conclusions about Pink Communism's prospects. It also serves the ancillary purpose of deepening readers' appreciation of the inherent deficiencies of Red, White, Golden and Pink Communisms.

Classic Liberal Democratic economic efficiency

Paretian optimality theory (the Liberal Democratic perfectly competitive ideal) illuminates the possibilities for Liberal Semi-Democratic and Pink Communist orders.[146] It sheds light on optimal education, training, factor allocation, technology choice, production, distribution, transfers, utility and well-being. The Paretian ideal can be relaxed to take account of imperfect competition and power,[147] and clarifies the comparative merit of Liberal Democratic and Pink Communist systems.

Five spaces warrant consideration: factor, production, distribution, transfer and well-being. The constructs in each space assume that transactors are rational (make consistent transitive choices) and maximize utility. If participants are freely competitive and sovereign without CPC subordination, outcomes will be Liberal Democratic ("Pareto ideal"). The people's preferences will dominate the CPCs. If the CPC instills its preferences in the people, then outcomes can be ideal from both the Pink Communist and Liberal Democratic perspectives. In all other cases, where state and private preferences are incompatible, and/or competition is incomplete, results must be Pareto inferior.[148]

Figure 6.1 illustrates Liberal Democratic and Pink Communist production possibilities. The coordinate axes forming the sides of the Edgeworth–Bowley box represent equilibrium supplies of capital (k) and labor (l). The sides end where the utility from work (derived consumption) is just equal to the foregone value of leisure.

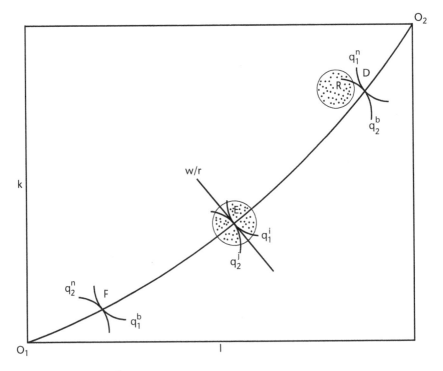

FIGURE 6.1 Factor allocation.

The Edgeworth–Bowley box contains all possible allocations of labor and capital in the production of the two goods (q_1) and (q_2) shown at the lower and upper intersection of coordinate axes (their origins). The space also contains two nested, convex, radial sets of isoquants [production functions: $q = F(k, l)$], one for each good. These are the best technologies in the sense that they maximize profits and individual utilities. The value of the superscripts on every isoquant (unit level of production) is the highest competitively attainable. The farther any isoquant lies from its respective origin, the higher the output level.

If an economy is in a state of total utility-maximizing equilibrium, there must be one corresponding point inside the Edgeworth–Bowley box. This point represents the utility-optimizing supply assortment, and the maximum output consistent with it. If output were below potential, or in the wrong mix, then the utility-maximizing process would be incomplete. The equilibrium point in Figure 6.1 is the isoquant double tangency (point E) because production at other points along either isoquant would mean that the economy could produce more q_1 or q_2 without lowering the output of the other. The price line at all double tangencies is the wage–rental ratio. The only utility-optimizing wage–rental ratio is the one that holds at complete equilibrium point E.

It is also possible to imagine a set of Pareto equilibria for alternative configurations of factor and product demand (caused by a change of individual taste). These counterfactual alternatives entail minor adjustments of the sides of the Edgeworth–Bowley box (not shown), and correspond with other general equilibrium isoquant double tangencies. The contract curve is the set of all efficient factor supply, input allocation and production points, actual or counterfactual. It represents a menu of actual and potential Liberal Democratic optimal outputs (Gross Domestic Products [GDPs]).[149] The locus is useful because it allows us to visualize the characteristics of Liberal Democratic and Pink Communist efficient economies. Any point other than E along the contract curve, like D or F, is inferior to the Liberal Democratic approach because the goods supplied do not maximize consumer utility. The outputs at D and F could be ideal (in both the Liberal Democratic and Pink Communist cases) if the actual demand pattern were different, but it is not. Of course, if the economy operated at point R, off the contract curve, it would be more Pareto inferior because factor misallocation means that a competitive individualist society could have done better by sliding down the isoquant to point D, increasing the production of one good, while holding the supply of the other fixed. All counterfactual outcomes along the contract curve are "technically efficient" because even though consumers dis-prefer them, they could have been counterfactually ideal. All other points are technically and "economically inefficient" because they fail to maximize utility and minimize system-wide cost. E and only E is the true Pareto equilibrium.

This true Pareto equilibrium may be Liberal Democratic or Pink Communist as long as participants are autonomous.[150] It does not matter whether players are self-centered or socially conscious. Liberal Democratic and Pink Communist point E will be identical only in the unlikely event that liberal and communist individuals have the same tastes.

This is the theory. However, in practice, Chinese Pink Communism cannot be Pareto optimal because the CPC only tolerates leasehold property. Prohibiting freehold property restricts competition and thereby prevents Pink Communism from attaining point E.[151]

Output possibilities can be spotlighted by redrawing the contract curve in Figure 6.1 in the production space (Figure 6.2). The coordinate axes represent outputs q_1 and q_2 instead of the factors k and l. The space inside the coordinate axes contains the equilibrium production point E, and all counterfactual Pareto equilibria like D and F forming the contract curve in Figure 6.1. This locus derived in Figure 6.1 and remapped in the production space is called the production possibility frontier (PPF). As before, point E and only point E is a true Paretian equilibrium. Other points on the PPF are technically, but not economically, efficient unless they are based on the competitive, socially conscious choices of Pink Communist consumers.[152] All points inside the frontier are inefficient, although it can be said that points along the ray from the origin through E, other than E, are right assortments in the wrong volumes, and economically efficient in an inferior technical sense.

Pink Communist outcomes will be inefficient whenever socially conscious work (at egalitarian wages), consumption and leisure choices are coerced (forced substitution), and/or programs are state imposed against the people's will. Pink Communist coercion and/or mismanagement shift production from E to points elsewhere on or off the production possibilities frontier. These points will be technically and/or economically inefficient whenever they do not reflect ideal socially conscious Pink Communist preferences. When these norms are violated the dimensions of the Edgeworth–Bowley box in Figure 6.1 may be inferior (under- or over-supply of capital and labor); wages may be too egalitarian, inputs may be misallocated, technologies inferior, finance inappropriate, management incompetent and product

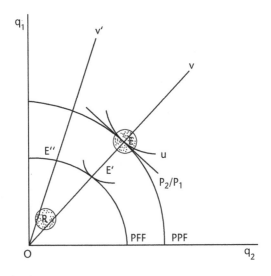

FIGURE 6.2 Production.

characteristics and assortments subpar. Isoquants will be suboptimal, the contract curve will be miscomputed and point E will be unattainable.[153]

Pink Communism for all these reasons, including the ban on freehold property, will operate below E′ or E″ in Figure 6.2, on a constrained production feasibility frontier (PFF). If Pink Communism is only slightly coercive, regulation is competent and state programs responsive to the people's will, technical and economic inefficiency will be small. The greater the coercion and poorer the regulation, the worse the result, with extreme cases like Red Communism illustrated by point R.[154] White Communism production should exceed point E′ because Xi Jinping prioritizes production over social justice. There is a tradeoff between maximizing output and optimizing social welfare.

The preceding analysis assumes perfect competition. This is an unrealistic standard, but is not fatal.[155] Analogous principles hold for imperfect competition. The circular subsets in Figures 6.1 and 6.2 illustrate the qualification by transforming point E and R into fuzzy sets.[156] The concepts of technical and economic inefficiency continue to apply, but their measurement in imperfectly competitive markets is less precise.[157]

Perfect production is a good start, but it is not enough. Consumers must maximize their utility by acquiring the best assortment of products their purses allow in wholesale and retail markets. Figure 6.3 illustrates how consumers competitively purchase goods manufactured in Figure 6.2, paid for from wages and other earned income. It takes the equilibrium outputs q_1 and q_2 (points E in Figures 6.1 and 6.2), and arrays them unit by unit along the coordinate axes. The endpoint of each axis

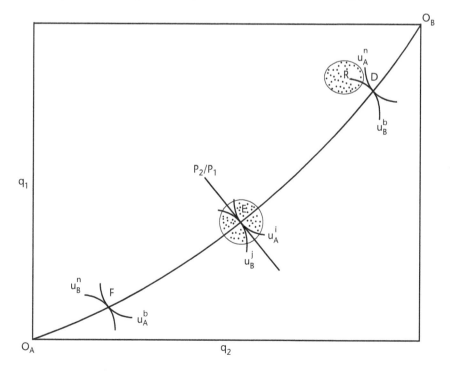

FIGURE 6.3 Retail.

represents the total amounts available for distribution between individuals A and B in the two-participant retail market. Points at the southwest and northeast vertices, and in the box's interior, represent feasible distributions of the goods between the parties, who are guided by their convex, nested ordinal indifference curves (iso-utility) radiating from the lower and upper origins [$U_A = G(q_1, q_2)$; $U_B = H(q_1, q_2)$].

If an economy is in a state of total utility-maximizing equilibrium, there must be one corresponding corner or inside point in the Edgeworth–Bowley distribution space. This point represents the utility-optimizing retail allocation of the Pareto ideal output supply because otherwise the utility-maximizing process would be incomplete. Shoppers achieve it through unfettered negotiation with each other, given the wages and rents earned by claimants A and B at the indifference curve double tangency (point E) in Figure 6.3. E is the general retail equilibrium point because distribution at any other point along either iso-utility curve would mean that one participant could increase his/her utility without reducing the other's utility, given the equilibrium income distribution. The price line P_2/P_1 at the double tangency E is the only true competitive Pareto price equilibrium. It could also represent the Pink Communist ideal if socially conscious consumption distribution is voluntary (no forced substitution), prices are not subsidized or fixed, and the state refrains from rationing.

Point E is the only Pareto-efficient distribution in the Edgeworth–Bowley box, but if tastes were different (given the same retail supplies), or there were post-production tax transfers altering the distribution of purchasing power, a locus of counterfactual communist Pareto-ideal distributions would be generated, represented by the contract curve in Figure 6.3. Just as in the production case, contract curve points other than E are technically efficient in the sense that the distribution could be ideal had competitive wages been different. Points off the contract curve however are always technically and economically inefficient because better outcomes are possible for one participant without reducing the utility of the other.

Pink Communism cannot attain point E in Figure 6.3 because by assumption the CPC compels consumers to purchase goods that they dis-prefer, prices are subsidized and/or products are rationed. Pink Communist distribution takes place instead at point D, F or R. Whitish-Pink Communist economies operate close to the contract curve, at points reflecting Xi's notion of social justice. Reddish-Pink Communist systems operate close to point R. The same basic inferences apply to imperfectly competitive Pink Communism as indicated by the fuzzy sets surrounding points E and R.

Tax transfers governed by analogous competitive principles are an important aspect of modern market systems. The utility depicted in Figure 6.4 remaps the physical distribution of goods q_1 and q_2 between participants A and B. The coordinate axes array ordinal iso-utilities in increasing order from the origin, and points within the space identify the iso-utility level attained by each comrade consuming his or her respective share of the retail distribution. The Pareto-optimal utility distribution is point E. If Pink Communists decide to improve social justice through efficient post-production tax transfers, the utility effects will be reflected along the utility possibilities frontier (UPF) to the right or left of point E.[158] If tax transfers are

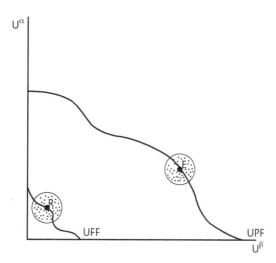

FIGURE 6.4 Utility.

performed inefficiently, Pink Communist utility outcomes will decline to a lower utility feasibilities frontier (UFF).[159]

Pink Communism cannot attain point E in Figure 6.4 because state intervention in the retail market (Figure 6.3) prevents the optimal result. Pink Communist distribution takes place instead at some other point along the UPF, or at a point below. Whitish-Pink Communist economies operate close to the UPF, at points reflecting Xi's notion of social justice. Reddish-Pink Communist systems operate close to point R on a UFF. The same basic deductions hold for imperfectly competitive versions of Pink Communism as indicated by the fuzzy sets surrounding points E and R.

It should be obvious that ordinal utility outcomes in Whitish-Pink and Reddish Pink Communist market systems are inferior from a Paretian individualist perspective. They are apt to be deficient from various socially conscious viewpoints too because of leasehold restrictions, and the imponderable difficulties of regulating wages and prices, rationing, tax transferring and Pink Communist public programming.

The supposition that national utility generated by Whitish-Pink Communism should exceed the Reddish-Pink benchmark also follows from the gap between points E and R displayed in Figure 6.4. Markets provide more national utility at every stage of the economic process than controlled economies.

Nonetheless, Red Communists can validly counter-argue that the litmus test for communist systems of all colors is well-being,[160] not utility. Economists define utility very narrowly. It pertains to the pleasure or psychological benefit individuals derive from consuming a unit of a good or service without consideration given to external benefits or costs. If a shot of vodka feels good, it is rational from a utilitarian standpoint to drink it down the hatch, and keep on drinking until it is no longer pleasurable regardless of individual and social side effects.

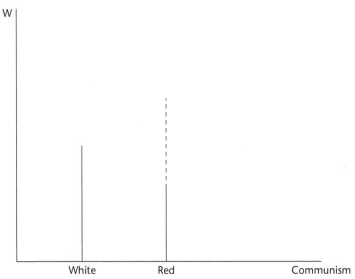

Solid lines represent material well-being

Hatched lines represent social well-being

FIGURE 6.5 Well-being.

Well-being by contrast includes utility as economists define it, but only as a subordinate aspect of individual and societal life quality. It is a holistic concept that combines the utility derived from chugalugging vodka with its side effects to judge individual and social satisfaction, fulfillment and contentment.[161]

Figure 6.5 clarifies the distinction. It compares Red and White Communist well-being from Mao's and Xi's perspective. Well-being (W) is arrayed on the ordinate, with the two communist systems on the abscissa. White Communist well-being as Xi perceives it depends solely on the utility derived from point R in Figure 6.3 indicated by the solid vertical line. Red Communist well-being in Mao's eyes includes utility (the solid portion of the Red Communist bar), and individual and societal external economies (equality, justice, harmony) too.[162] The well-being derived from the combination of the two effects makes Red greater than White Communist well-being, even though the GDP generated in Xi's system is superior.

This outcome is an example, not a proof. Utility and well-being are both subjective. They cannot be measured precisely, and are not strongly correlated with GDP. The claim that Red Communism offers China the prospect of superior well-being therefore is mostly an article of faith.[163]

Disequilibrium adjustment mechanism

Figures 6.1–6.4 illustrate the characteristics of general equilibria where Pink Communist participants exhaustively optimize their utility in work, production, distribution, transfers and other pursuits. These results are attained through extensive, rational negotiations with others influenced by prices (terms of exchange) and the requirements of profit maximization.

The search takes three basic forms depending on whether participants negotiate (compute) the exchange of stocks (including inventories and labor), or "flows" (currently produced goods/services). Both may involve profit-seeking, but in the case of stocks, price adjustment is primary. In the case of flows, output adjustment dominates.

The price negotiation process for stocks is called the Walrasian excess demand price adjustment mechanism, in honor of Leon Walras (1834–1910), an eminent nineteenth-century French general equilibrium theorist. It hypothesizes that if at any moment sellers perceive that their offer prices exceed buyers' willingness to pay (excess supply), leaving suppliers holding excess inventories, they will respond by reducing their offer price. If the discount proves insufficient, they will continue cutting prices until their inventory holdings are optimal. Should they over-discount, they will swiftly discover that their inventories are too low. At this point, they will probe buyers' willingness to bid by raising prices, continuing to do so until the quantity supplied and demanded are equal.

The decision rules are simple. The market price (p) at any instant (t) is specified to be a function (F) of the difference between the quantity (q) demanded (d), and the quantity supplied (s).

$$dp/dt = F(q^d - q^s) \qquad (6.1)$$

$$\text{If } q^d > q^s, \text{ then}$$

$$dp/dt > 0, \text{ and prices will rise.}$$

$$\text{If } q^d < q^s \text{ then}$$

$$dp/dt < 0, \text{ and prices will fall.}$$

Both processes will continue until $dp/dt = 0$, which will be a stable equilibrium because the adjustment mechanism is symmetric. Competitive utility searching automatically reduces excess demand and excess supply to zero.

Figure 6.6 provides a geometric version of the communist Walrasian process in the retail market. Price is arrayed on the ordinate, quantity along the abscissa. The demand curve is downward sloping in accordance with the principle of diminishing marginal utility. The supply curve slopes upward because the cost of stocking inventories increases with congestion. Consider the case where the retailer is overstocked at point A'.

The corresponding offer price is p_A, which intersects the demand curve at A. Supply q^s_A exceeds demand q^d_A, which according the communist Walrasian rule causes the retailer to discount.

Excess supply here diminishes, but the process is not complete. Discounting continues to E, where the quantities demanded and supplied are equal. If the retailer overshoots the mark, and over-discounts, the Pink Communist Walrasian process will work in reverse, with prices rising until E.

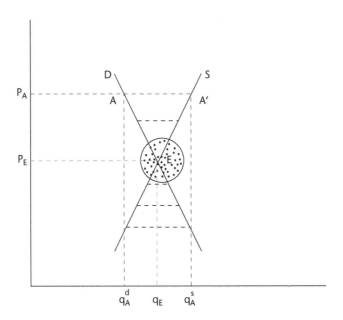

FIGURE 6.6 Price adjustment.

The Pink Communist Walrasian excess demand price adjustment mechanism reallocates capital and labor from R in Figure 6.1 to D. The wage rate at R is too low relative to the rental rate on capital. This creates excess demand for labor, which raises the wage, making it the same for both employers. D is a counterfactual, not a true competitive equilibrium, so the process is incomplete. Profit-seeking will compel the first output activity to contract, and the second to expand.

The Pink Communist Walrasian excess demand price adjustment mechanism also applies in Figure 6.3. Here bidding raises the price of good q_2, redistributing the assortment of retail supplies from R to D, which again is a counterfactual equilibrium point. Then the ability of individuals A and B to pay, given their budget constraints derived from earned income in Figure 6.1, brings about the full equilibrium at E. There is no new production in the retail diagram. The goods sold in Figure 6.3 are those that were actually produced in Figure 6.2.

Clearly, Pink Communist Walrasian price adjustment has broad scope, but it does not govern production. Prices also may vary in determining optimal supplies, but the driving force in the competitive model is profit maximization. As before, market participants strive to augment their utility, but do so indirectly by increasing income (profit) and wealth. This process is called the Marshallian excess price quantity adjustment mechanism after the British economist Alfred Marshall (1840–1924). In the most general case, manufacturers know the buyers' demand curve. This allows them to compare the demand price that they face for every level of production with the firm's corresponding unit cost. The difference is the excess price, that is, unit profit, computed as the difference between unit revenue and cost.

The firm's decision rule is elementary. The quantity supplied (q) at any instant (t) is specified to be a function (G) of the difference between the demand price (p^d) and the unit production cost (p^s).

$$dq/dt = G(p^d - p^s) \qquad (6.2)$$

If $p^d > p^s$, then

$dq/dt > 0$, and firms will expand production.

If $p^d < p^s$, then

$dq/dt < 0$, and managers will curtail production.

Both process will continue until $dq/dt = 0$, which will be a stable equilibrium because the adjustment mechanism is symmetric. Both excess quantities demanded, and excess quantities supplied, diminish to zero through a competitive utility/profit maximization search.

Figure 6.7 provides a geometric version of the communist Marshallian process in manufacturing. Price is arrayed on the ordinate, quantity along the abscissa. The demand curve is downward sloping, reflecting buyers' diminishing marginal utility. The supply curve slopes upward because the marginal physical productivity of inputs (valued at fixed prices) is a diminishing function of output. Consider the case where the firm discovers that for the achieved production level the demand price p^d_A at A exceeds the supply price (marginal cost) p^s_A at A'.

The vertical difference means that the firm makes a unit profit, and according to the Marshallian rule expands production. A recalculation of the demand price and

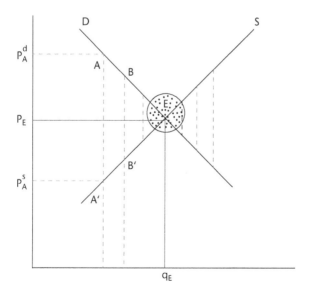

FIGURE 6.7 Quantity adjustment.

supply cost reveals that unit profit remains positive, and the search proceeds to q_E, where unit revenue (price) exactly equals unit supply cost. If the manager over-shoots the mark, expanding production beyond E, the Pink Communist Marshallian process will work in reverse. The firm will discover that it is losing money on the production of each unit beyond q_E, and will return to E.

The conventional geometry of profit maximization illustrated in Figure 6.8 con-firms the soundness of the communist Marshallian principle. The variables on the ordinate and abscissa are the same, but an infinitely elastic marginal revenue curve replaces the downward-sloping demand curve in accordance with the perfectly competitive assumption that small firms cannot influence market prices. A marginal cost curve substitutes for the Pink Communist Marshallian supply curve, and an average total cost curve is added for completeness. Suppose as earlier that before equilibrium is achieved at point E, marginal revenue (A) exceeds marginal cost (A′). The difference between MR and MC is a unit profit that will encourage the firm to expand. Once again, unit profit is positive, and the manager will continue probing until equilibrium (profit maximization) is achieved at E. If there is a mis-calculation, and the enterprise expands output beyond E, a marginal loss will occur, prompting a return to E. The Pink Communist Marshallian principle and profit maximization thus are the same thing, yielding the familiar conclusion that profit seeking governs managerial action in competitive economies.

Specifically, the Pink Communist Marshallian excess price quantity adjustment mechanism drives both firms in Figure 6.1 to produce optimal assortments and volumes of their respective goods. If production occurs at the counterfactual opti-mum D, profit-seeking will sequentially expand production in firm 2 and reduce in firm 1 until the true equilibrium is achieved at E. Likewise, firms operating on

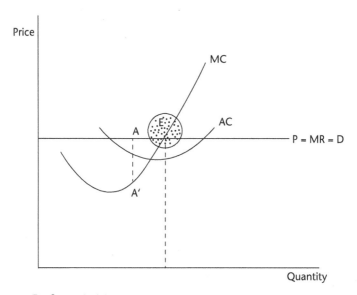

FIGURE 6.8 Profit maximizing.

production feasibility frontiers in Figure 6.2 will expand output along any vector until they reach the production possibility frontier, and then shift to E by Walrasian and Marshallian processes.

The invisible hand is the combination of both automatic adjustment mechanisms, or the Pink Communist equilibrating process can be interpreted as two-handed: one Walrasian, the other Marshallian, often operating interactively.

The power of competitive economic theory lies in its existence theorems, which demonstrate the possibility of attaining E in Figures 6.1–6.4, and 6.6–6.8, under Pink and White Communism, and further in the efficacy of the invisible hand. Red Communist planning often is said to be as good or better than the invisible hand, but this is false. Although the duality theorem demonstrates that perfect planning and perfect competition mathematically yield the same result,[164] this conceals the fact that planning and administration in practice are less effective than Pink Communist imperfect competition.[165] Mao's commands cannot outshine Adam Smith's invisible hand because planners, system directors and administrators do not have reliable real-time information about enterprise productions functions and consumer utility functions, and lack a lucid understanding of their own decision functions,[166] which together with the deficiencies of state freehold ownership and authoritarianism are the hallmarks of Red Communist inferiority.

The analysis of Pink Communism can be broadened to include the dynamic effects of investment, technology choice and long-term growth. The exercise reveals that optimal investment, technology choice and long-term growth are achievable under Pink Communism, but inferior outcomes are more likely because Reddish-Pink Communists prioritize social justice, and Whitish Pink Communists maximize rather than optimize long-term growth. Both biases are incompatible with optimization. As Irving Fisher (1867–1947) taught, investment is a device that allows people to trade with the future. People do not simply invest. They forego current consumption to enjoy an expanded stream of future income in accordance with their time preference, or borrow to consume today, repaying out of future income. Either way, the Pareto ideal results require people to optimize their utility and well-being rather than fixate on dynamically maximizing equality or wealth. Bounded rational restrictions qualify this judgment of best Pink Communist possibilities, as do the omission of variables like power-seeking, willfulness, well-being, fulfillment and contentment. However, just as in the static imperfectly competitive paradigm, the presumption that Red Communism is inferior holds undiminished.[167]

It follows directly that the Chinese leaders do not have to choose between Red and White Communism. They have a wide spectrum of Pink static and dynamic alternatives. Wise Beijing rulers should select the shade of pink that maximizes national well-being from the people's perspective.[168] Reddish systems offer the people more social justice and lower living standards, Whitish systems higher per capita income and lower equality.

PART IV
Beyond Communism

7

LIBERAL DEMOCRACY

Classic Liberal Democracy is Golden Communism's principal rival.[169] It offers nations the possibility of adopting a Pareto-optimal economic system that mobilizes initiative, maximizes productivity, pays people exactly what they earn and allows them to maximize their utility. Golden Liberal Democracy enthrones the individual over society. Consumers and voters are sovereign. They can be as charitable or selfish as they prefer. They can hire government as an agent to provide public services, or do everything themselves, all in accordance with the social contract and rule of law. Adam Smith and John Locke are their patron saints.[170]

Perfectly competitive Golden Liberal Democracy does not require world government. It is a pluralist vision within and among nations. Individuals are free to migrate, invest, transfer technology, produce, trade, distribute and transfer. Figures 6.1–6.8 hold throughout for domestic and international economic activity with a few minor adjustments. The sides of the Edgeworth–Bowley factor-production box in Figure 6.1 may increase or decrease due to labor and capital migration, and technology transfer may increase isoquant superscripts. The sides of the Edgeworth–Bowley retail distribution box in Figure 6.3 may increase or decrease due to net imports and the new Pareto equilibrium point E in Figure 6.1. Transfer possibilities in Figure 6.4 and well-being in Figure 6.5 likewise will require some fine-tuning, but none of this is fundamental. The core principles of exhaustive utility and profit maximizing hold domestically before and after international trade. The Golden Liberal Democratic ideal as the textbooks and Heckscher–Olin theory teach is an individualist multinational utopia.[171] It is comprehensively efficient, maximizes individual utility worldwide without world government, and is the essence of the American Dream.[172]

Perfectly competitive Golden Liberal Democracy, like Golden Communism, is impossible both in its national and international idealizations. Bounded rationality prevents individuals from exhaustively maximizing profits and utility in the private sector and Kenneth Arrow has shown that voters' demand cannot precisely control public services.[173] Nations have to settle for imperfectly competitive Liberal Democracy. Figures 6.1–6.4 and 6.6–6.8 show that workably competitive Liberal Democracy can perform very well, but perfection is out of the question.

Real Liberal Democracy comes in a variety of colors and shades.[174] White Liberal Democracy puts self-centered individuals on top. Red Liberal Democracy operates the other way round. Red individuals are altruistic. They are concerned mostly with the needs of others. Real Liberal Democracies today are Pink. They are blends of white and red across the selfish–altruist spectrum. White Liberal Democracies are synonymous with laissez-fare capitalism; Red Liberal Democracies are compassionate.

This classification mimics the Pink Communist spectrum, but the correspondence is inexact because the government in all Pink Liberal Democratic systems is an agent, not a sovereign ruler. It does not impose its will on economic actors in society's name. Liberal Democracy is supposed to treat everyone equally under the rule of law. The state should never privilege some over others against the will of victims, but Liberal Democracies (especially in social democracies) often flout the rule. When this occurs, they become illiberal in varying degrees.

Donald Trump's American populist ideal is a light Pink Liberal Democratic regime.[175] It blends individualism, competition, entrepreneurship, tolerance, equal opportunity, an open society and democracy with some compassionate social protection. Trump advocates limited tariff protection for American workers and supports a panoply of social programs costing trillions of dollars as long as they do not infringe constitutionally protected property and civic rights.[176] Former President Barack Obama's American Dream was an Illiberal Democratic model because it contained a contentious Red social agenda that shredded constitutional equal rights protections, privileging some over others in society's name.[177]

The Pareto efficiency characteristics of Pink Liberal Democracy make it superior to Pink Communism from an individualist perspective. Illiberal Democracies suffer from the same deficiencies as Pink Communist counterparts. When the state overrides basic property and civic rights in the name of "noble" causes, some must always unjustly suffer. White Communists exploit workers and peasants; Red Illiberal Democrats abuse the middle class.

Illiberal Democracy today is the norm, not the exception.[178] Western Social Democrats resemble Reddish-Pink Communists more than they care to acknowledge. The gap between White Communists and Pink Liberal Democrats is wide, but the Reddish-Pink Communist and Pink Illiberal Democratic divide is narrow.

Chinese and Western economic systems can remain poles apart or can converge in various ways. Xi can move right to Trump by abolishing China's ban on freehold property, or left to Angela Merkel by reddening his core White Communist regime. The merit of these realignments cannot be judgment inclusively by "technical efficiency." It involves complex subjective judgments about well-being that lie in the eyes of the beholder.[179]

Nonetheless, "technical efficiency" does provide some guidance. Figures 6.1–6.8 suggest that China would benefit more by transitioning from White Communist to Liberal Democracy than Illiberal Democracy of any hue. Illiberal alternatives are half-a-loaf solutions. They deserve consideration, but do not assure improved well-being.

The good news is that there are no theoretical barriers preventing Xi from reforming Chinese market communism across a broad Pink spectrum from White to Red, or transitioning from market communism to Liberal Democracy in baby steps via Illiberal Democracy.

The impediments are practical: political risks and social dangers. Shifts along the Pink Communist spectrum create winners and losers, spark conflict and jeopardize CPC rule. Nudging White Communists left will be a hard sell, and persuading the CPC to dissolve itself will be far more daunting, even if the Chinese people overwhelming agree that transition is the right thing to do.

8

GLOBALISM

Liberal Democracy is a pluralist vision within and among nations, often conflated with globalization, misconceived as ever-expanding international commerce, migration, capital mobility and technology transfer. Pareto efficient Liberal Democracy optimizes participant's utility. It does not maximize foreign trade activity.[180]

Liberal Democratic regimes permit illiberal ones to participate in their markets on a satisficing basis. Beijing seized the opportunity with gusto after the World Trade Organization (WTO) approved China's membership in 2001. The trade has been mutually beneficial, and had an additional advantage for the CPC. There were no political strings attached. Xi Jinping was not compelled to modify White Communism's economic and social characteristics to please China's trade partners.

This mutual political tolerance persisted even though globalization gradually became more and more illiberal, and shifted left.[181] The shift is reflected in the international relations literature by the term "globalist,"[182] which means an illiberal hegemonic world order with a social justice and privileged business agenda.[183] In recent decades, the boundaries between America and foreign nations have dissolved into the idea that the United States as the fountainhead of globalization should become the indispensable "global nation."[184] This oxymoron means that America should transform its culture into a progressive international blend, cede some of its national sovereignty to transnational institutions and impose its universalized system on the world. Most Democrats and Republicans are globalizers. They desire to rule the world from Washington in the name of all the planet's improved homogenized peoples, instead of the people they actually represent. The globalist posture gives them more degrees of freedom in pursuing their declaratory and hidden agendas at home and abroad.

European social democrats and the American Obama administration spearheaded globalism,[185] with one negative consequence for China. Globalists relentlessly sought to increase the West's control over the gains from trade by constructing a transnational commercial and financial juggernaut.[186] Xi Jinping complained and strove to augment China's influence in the World Bank, the IMF and other transnational institutions with some success, but China was still less well off than it would have been under a global Liberal Democratic order.

Donald Trump's presidency threatens to upset the applecart, inflicting direct economic costs on China, together with a tantalizing mix of indirect economic gains and political risks. He intends to impose a 45 percent tariff on Chinese exports to prod Beijing into granting American exporters unfettered access to China's domestic market.[187] This will hurt some CPC insiders. However, he also wants America to withdraw from transnational organizations. Trump has already scuttled the Trans-Pacific Partnership. This will reduce America's hegemonic rents and provide the CPC with an opportunity to capture its own hegemonic rents by strengthening its position as a co-globalist leader.[188] Xi has already declared his intention to try,[189] but the gambit may not be a free lunch. The Europeans will press the CPC vigorously to democratize and accept a Red Communist social justice agenda. If Xi is nimble enough, he may be able to have his cake and eat it.

He may be able to transform China into a global White Communist hegemon on his own terms, without making concessions to the Reds. This would constitute a major transformation of China's communist system, shifting from a domestic to a global White Communist paradigm.[190] If he fails, Reds within the CPC may gain the upper hand, jeopardizing global communist power.

It appears for the moment that Xi is game, that he will seize the opportunity provided by Donald Trump's anti-transnationalism to displace America as globalist hegemon.[191] There is no economic downside to the strategy; but there are significant domestic political risks. If Xi advocates democracy and social justice in his transnational role, Reddish-Pink Communists could press aggressively for the same reforms home. It may be wiser from a White Communist standpoint to let sleeping furies lie.[192]

9

CONFUCIUS

Xi's pursuit of prosperity and great national power has distanced Chinese White Communism from its idealist egalitarian and social justice roots. There is little of Marx's ideology left to prevent Beijing from abandoning communism entirely and switching sides. The leadership only has to set its mind on relinquishing the Communist Party's monopoly on political power, disassociate itself explicitly from the working class and peasantry, repudiate economic and social equality, decriminalize freehold private property and base rewards on the value of services rendered. It can do these things candidly, or double-talk.

Switching sides means taking the "capitalist" road, but the concept of "capitalism" is ambiguous. Capitalism is plural, not singular. Freehold private property and for-profit enterprise distinguish capitalism from other "isms," but they do not fully define the concept. Capitalism may have other important characteristics. It can be democratic or authoritarian. It can be perfectly competitive, workably competitive, oligopolistic or monopolistic. It can be liberal or illiberal. Illiberal capitalism can favor the rich, poor or special social interests.

If Xi decides to ditch White Communism, he must choose the replacement that he likes best. The simplest option would be to replace White Communism with White Illiberal Autocracy. The two models are close substitutes. He can accomplish this by decriminalizing freehold private property, or more courageously selecting White Illiberal Democracy. Xi need not be too bold. Democracy does not have to mean true Lockean democracy.[193] A one-party controlled democracy with balloting like Vladimir Putin's sovereign democracy might arguably suffice.[194]

If Xi's primary concern is the well-being of the Chinese people, he should consider a well-functioning version of Pink Liberal or Illiberal Democracy investigated in Chapter 6. He can weigh the tradeoffs between efficiency and equity, and choose accordingly.

However, there is another option that the CPC might find appealing – Confucian Liberal Democracy.[195] The model is Liberal Democracy with Confucian Chinese characteristics.[196] It has all the Pareto efficiency properties displayed in Figures 6.1–6.8, but maximizes the utility and well-being of Confucian family units, instead of the utility and well-being of autonomous individuals. Confucian Liberal Democracy is not as efficient as pure Liberal Democracy from an individualist perspective, but has compensating virtues from Xi's point of view. It makes the nuclear and extended family responsible for guiding and protecting its members; and it promotes loyalty to the regime's leader and self-sacrifice for the nation. Confucian Liberal Democracy makes everyone better off than they are under White Communism, except the ruling party, which would suffer a reduction in its arbitrary powers. Confucian deference gives elected regime officials more authority than a Lockean democracy, but China's leaders would be more vulnerable to popular censure than they are now.

The family unit is interesting because members have fewer degrees of freedom than do autonomous individuals.[197] This is why Confucian Liberal Democracy is intrinsically less efficient than Liberal Democracy from an individual utilitarian perspective. Dad, mom, brother and sister do not individually control the family purse, and myriad obligations restrict their behavior. Family well-being is unitary, not fully separable. Families are micro-economies with private (individual) and public (family) sectors. Members act as individual utility maximizers in some activities, but the unit collectively decides how to manage the public good (external benefits and costs) for the family's wellbeing.[198] The family determines whether dad, mom, son and daughter vacation together, or save the vacation money for daughter's college education.

If the family unit wisely manages the public good, everyone may be better off even though individual utility maximizing is restricted because the family takes proper account of interdependent utilities and external economies. This makes well-run families attractive, and mismanaged families unappealing.

Individuals in Liberal Democracies have the right to choose whether to operate independently or within families. They select the option that maximizes their utility in the competitive paradigm. Confucian Liberal Democracies deny them this option. They ban fully autonomous individualism, prescribe the family order and mandate family well-being as society's highest goal.

The concept of family varies across cultures. Each type has a different impact on the possibilities of familial well-being. The Confucian ideal is hierarchical. Every member of the Confucian nuclear family has an assigned role. Dad sits atop the pecking order. He chairs the family micro-economy and is the final arbiter. Mom runs the household. The husband and wife are jointly responsible for inculcating their children with Confucian moral precepts. They also cooperatively decide each child's career assignment and education, and establish a management regime where the eldest son supervises his younger brothers down a chain of command, and the eldest daughter does the same for junior sisters. Confucian precepts instruct all members to cheerfully subordinate their personal desires to the family good and relish the pleasures of familial bonding and harmony.

The same scheme applies to the extended family, neighboring families, up the chain to the emperor who is the ultimate patriarch. The vision offers the promise of perfect well-being, prosperity and harmony all under the wise and benevolent guidance of the imperial ruler.

Confucian precepts (aphoristic rules of ethical conduct) universally govern behavior, but they are not surrogates for the market. Chinese individual and families are free to maximize profits in production and utility in consumption in accordance with Figures 6.1–6.8. Confucianism makes the family well-being the goal of market participants, and establishes the rules of market conduct, but Confucian Liberal Democracies are otherwise comprehensively competitive.

Confucian Liberal Democracy instills the nation with the spirit of self-reliance within the family network, kinship, communal duty, transgenerational continuity, respectability, beneficence, mutual support, financial prudence, competitiveness and prosperity seeking. Righteous precepts in this scheme prevent despotism. Family units self-motivate and self-police from below without the self-centeredness many believe contaminates Liberal Democracy. A Confucian China would offer the nation expanded property rights, increased equality, greater personal freedom and values more compatible with Chinese tradition than the imported ideals of Western communism, Enlightenment and post-modernism.

The cornerstone of the ideal social order for Confucians of every persuasion is a set of moral precepts inculcated from birth intended to promote personal, communal, societal and national harmony, without higher legal, imperial, transcendental or divine guidance. The approach (conscience and duty) is the antithesis of Qin Shi Huang's top-down governance,[199] predicated on blind obedience to imperial edicts and administrative laws ("legalism"). [200]

Confucianism teaches that every individual's supreme moral obligation is promoting familial (dynastic) well-being, not God, country, administrative law or Kantian categorical imperatives. Familial duty is the summa bonum,[201] not individual centered conscience or the merit of specific outcomes ("consequentialism").[202] This makes Confucius an institutionalist. Well-being in Confucius's governance scheme is intrinsic to the orderly performance of the familial ballet, and does not depend on individuals realizing their human potentials. Confucians, of course, claim that faithful performance of choreographed familial duty is a prerequisite for individual psychological well-being, reflected in self-perceptions of fulfillment and contentment.

Confucius's ethics, as distinct from Confucian praxis, are broadly sound. Men and women avoid treating others badly to discourage retaliation (the "silver rule").[203] People should never harm other people by being hurtful, discourteous, imperious, dishonest, deceptive, false, envious, rancorous, manipulative, seductive, obscene, bawdy, treacherous, impious, unjust or malicious. They should not conspire, inveigle, traduce, slander, demean, debase, degrade, embarrass, humiliate, steal, burgle, defile, profane, injure, pillage, kidnap, seduce, molest, rape, torture or murder. Instead, they should be enlightened (educated), refined, cultured, discreet, polite, thoughtful, fair, benevolent, considerate, compassionate, generous, philanthropic, chaste, loyal, trustworthy, prudent, hardworking, frugal, farsighted, provident and wise. These behaviors, which are echoed by the Protestant Ethic, advance familial well-being by avoiding conflicts and vendettas, promoting prosperity, respect, friendship, love, peace, serenity, harmony, prosperity and happiness.

Confucian virtue is its own reward, and a benefice to society, just as it was for Plato.[204] There cannot be full well-being without moral integrity. Those who do good deeds benefit from their benevolence, and serve further as paragons for those who cannot find their bearings. They enable the less worthy, and lost souls to perceive the folly of their transgressions, and save themselves.

Confucian societies build on these ethical pillars by instilling senses of guilt for wrongdoing, and shame for disgraceful conduct that transform ethical precepts into a self-regulating familial and communitarian order. Plato's Republic mimics Confucius's moral logic, but relies on the righteous behavior of autonomous individuals clustered in three estates: philosopher kings (wisdom), warriors (courage) and commoners (temperance). Their collective action, instead of Confucian families and communities, jointly insure prosperity, security, national welfare and justice.

Confucius also invokes the notion of sage emperor (philosopher king), responsible for guiding his flock, but argues explicitly that familial and communitarian rectitude is a precondition for effective, virtuous state governance. Emperors in Confucius's universe, as heads of the national family, need only promulgate their benevolent programs, and inform their subjects, who then will loyally and harmoniously comply.

There is no place in the orthodox Confucian paradigm, or even Hsiung Shih-li's (1887–1968) neo-idealist Confucianism, which blends Confucian ritual with Buddhist ethics for individualistic self-discovery, fulfillment and minority empowerment.[205] Fung Yu-lan's neo-rationalist (Kantian) Confucianism combining Cheng-Chu's Song dynasty teachings with neo-realist philosophy incorporates some westernizing values,[206] but his Confucian outlook remains staunchly conservative, despite concessions to social mobility and socialism. The Confucian family is not just an ethical and efficient institution for getting things done. It gives meaning to individual existence and enriches the lives of all its members.

Confucian households are hierarchical. Everyone has a fixed role. Fathers rule and are guardians of family welfare. Women bear children and perform sundry chores. Children obey their parents, and care for them in their dotage. Everyone respects ancestors, and is filially pious, loyal and self-sacrificing for the greater family good. The hierarchy defines status. Husbands as wise lords and protectors are the most revered. Wives follow behind a distant second, appreciated by their husbands and esteemed by their children, an arrangement reminiscent of Thomas More's Utopia.[207]

No one lives for him or herself, or seeks personal fulfillment at the family's and nation's expense. Selfish behavior for Confucians, commonplace in the West and increasingly observable in overseas Chinese communities, is immoral. It creates disharmonies that poison human relations, debase familial well-being, generate adversarial productive regimes and impair productivity, spawning inequalities, strife and injustice. Just as in Plato's and More's universes, there exists one and only one ideal moral socio-economic system requiring everyone to know his or her place, and faithfully fulfill assigned roles.

Some may agree, but many Chinese do not see things this way. They challenge the idea that indoctrination, discipline, subordination, self-abnegation, self-sacrifice and loyalty really are individually and socially best because reliance on precepts implies that people do not think things through for themselves; they simply obey. Obedience is virtuous in some contexts, but not necessarily in others. Contemporary women and children may find Confucian obligations stifling, even though men might yearn for paradise lost. Female, male and juvenile misfits could adjust their attitudes under duress, but if they acquiesced, they would forego maximizing their well-being. Thus, even if people were morally compliant in Confucius's system, they might be unfulfilled and discontent.

These shortcomings apply with still greater force in the imperfect world mortals inhabit where people may espouse Confucian virtue, but play by very different rules. Husbands may be despots, wives conniving and children vicious. Family units may advance themselves by preying on other families, and disregard their communitarian obligations. Nepotism and corruption may be endemic. Communities may be rigidly divided into respected estates [Shi (scholars), Nong (peasants), Gong (craftsmen) and Shang (commerce)] and outcasts (soldiers, entertainers, prostitutes, etc.) under the supervision of emperors and nobles. The educated, especially those serving the imperial bureaucracy, may be privileged at the expense of businesspersons, workers and peasants. Fortunes are determined by birth, gender and ethnicity rather than ability because mobility across occupations and within families and communities is blocked. Greed and power may take precedence over harmony and justice. These degenerate circumstances turn Confucianism upside down.

Having started as a strategy for creating a virtuous, prosperous and harmonious society founded on ethically guided familial institutions, Confucius's teachings end up as a rationale for corruption, privilege and subjugation. Instead of promoting material progress and national well-being, Confucianism entrenches a corrupt order. China's inferior economic performance from 1500 to 1950, including Chiang Kaishek's nationalist Confucian interlude (1934–50) exemplifies the danger, while Taiwan's experience from 1950 to 2017 highlights the possibilities of constructive Confucian adaptation.

The merit of Confucian Liberal Democracy as a replacement for White Communism therefore partly depends on whether Confucianism can accommodate contemporary needs for personal freedom, and can deter corruption. Confucian Liberal Democracy should be more efficient than White Communism because it permits freehold private property and popular preferences democratically determine state programs, but this advantage may be offset by the danger of corruption, and normative judgments about personal freedom.

Corruption does not appear to be a deal breaker. The evidence suggests that Confucian Liberal Democracy is less corrupt than Xi's White Communism. Although corruption is notoriously difficult to measure, White Communist China appears more corrupt than Sinic nations with strong Confucian cultural influences. Xi's regime has a very low score on Transparency International's 2015 "virtuous conduct" index. On a scale from 1 to 165, China holds the 83rd position behind Singapore (8th) Hong Kong (18th) and Taiwan (30th).[208]

Fears about stifled personal freedom in Confucian Liberal Democratic systems also seem exaggerated. Few family members in Confucian households across the Sinic community today strictly adhere to the traditional norms. Birth order and gender restrictions have softened and patriarchic power has diminished. Notions of appropriate conduct have become more flexible, allowing Confucians to coexist with their contemporaries in a multi-cultural milieu comfortably. Women have more educational and professional opportunities, nearly on a par with men, and enjoy considerable personal liberty. The differences between the lifestyles of Confucians and the larger cosmopolitan world mostly are attributable to the high value Confucians place on family bonding and duty. Behavior that perturbs or subverts the nuclear family unit and larger familial networks still is deemed immoral.

Tables 9.1 through 9.5 document the statistic impact of these changes on Confucian family structure in Taiwan. The traditional Confucian preference for large families has shifted to smaller units, often with only a single child, and increasingly toward families with no children at all. Fertility rates have fallen and family units have aged (grayed). The proportion of three or more generation households has declined, while single-person households have steadily increased, driven in part by rising divorce rates and single-parent families (Tables 9.3 and 9.4). Female employment outside the household has increased substantially for both single and married women (Table 9.5), due variously to improved educational attainment, shifting public attitudes and reduced reliance on the patriarch's earning power.

TABLE 9.1 Graying of Taiwan's population (percent of population over 65)

1980	1990	2000	2006	2007
4	6	9	10	10.2

Source: Council for Economic Planning and Development. Projections of the Population for Taiwan Area and Taiwan Statistical Data Book, 2008.

TABLE 9.2 Fertility rate in Taiwan, 1960–2003 (percent)

1960–65	1985–90	1995–2000	2003	2007	2008
3.59	1.63	1.39	1.01	0.89	0.62

Source: Council for Economic Planning and Development. Projections of the Population for Taiwan Area, 2008.

TABLE 9.3 Taiwanese family structure (percent)

	1990	2000
Nuclear	60	55
Three generations	25	16
Single	13	21

Source: National Statistics, Directorate General of Budget, Accounting and Statistics, Executive Yuan.

TABLE 9.4 Divorce rates in Taiwan (percent)

1980	2000	2006	2007
8	24	28	26

Source: National Statistics, Directorate General of Budget, Accounting and Statistics, Executive Yuan.

TABLE 9.5 Female labor market participation rates (percent)

	1979	1980	2000	2006
All women	32	33	50	53
Married woman	29	31	35	34

Source: National Statistics, Directorate General of Budget, Accounting and Statistics, Executive Yuan.

Gains in personal freedom have come at a price. Family size decreased as women entered the labor force, and divorces increased. Fewer households provided shelter for the elderly, and the need for state social services has mushroomed.[209]

These losses, however, did not prevent Confucian Liberal Democracy from flourishing in other respects. Taiwan's Confucian modernization has paid handsome dividends. Economic growth has been superior in line with Asia's other "Tigers" or Four Little Dragons,[210] and like Japan, Taiwan produces high-quality exports driven by continuous technological progress, disciplined trade unions and cooperative labor-management relations. Social mobility and entrepreneurship have increased,[211] and the state has filled the social security void left by defamilization.[212]

Inequality has also plummeted. The Gini coefficient fell from 0.56 to 0.3 between 1953 and 1980, just the reverse of communist Chinese experience under Deng Xiaoping and Jiang Zemin.

During the 1990s, the government increased the size and scope of social welfare programs, allowing families to lighten their obligations to elder care, education and unemployment assistance. It also provided coverage for those living outside familial safety nets, including disadvantaged groups, supported some feminist aspirations, and had the further effect of transferring income from the rich to the poor. The government established national health insurance targeted at the elderly, children and the disabled and handicapped in 1985–91. It tackled unemployment insurance in 1994 and gender issues like juvenile prostitution and sexual assault in 1995–97, before invading the sanctity of the Confucian household with legislation on domestic violence prevention and assistance to women and households in difficulty in 1998–2000. A gender equality employment law was passed in 2002 to ameliorate the Confucian preference for male workers.[213]

Although democracy is still adolescent, having only started in 1987, it deepened thereafter with a series of successful multiparty elections, and civic participation has become vibrant.[214] Confucians take credit for all these positive developments, and may well deserve it.

Xi Jinping does not have to look westward to replace White Communism with a better system. China's party leaders can take their cue from the Four Little Dragons of the East, if the CPC does not choke swallowing its pride.

10

CHOOSING SIDES

China's technocratic White Communist market economic system works. It has provided high employment (4 percent unemployment), low inflation (2 percent per annum) and rapid economic growth (7 percent per annum), and has made China a great international power, but there are also many reasons for concern. The system is undemocratic and socially unjust. Development has been regionally uneven and growth is decelerating. Urban centers are congested, environmental pollution is endemic and some believe that a catastrophic financial crisis is looming just around the corner.

The CPC is aware of all these problems and claims to be addressing them vigorously at the policy level. Xi's "One-Road, One-Belt" initiative exemplifies the party's policy resolve. Is this sufficient, or should the CPC also consider system reform and transition possibilities? The right answer is yes to both options. The CPC should do so, if it wants to maximize China's well-being.

The best approach is simple. The CPC should clarify its priorities and then chose the system that maximizes China's well-being. This requires decisions about privileges and priorities. Well-being has a large individual component. Does the CPC want to maximize the well-being of every citizen? Does it favor some groups, and if so to what extent should they be privileged? The CPC must fully specify its objective function. It cannot determine the optimal system if it does not do so. Economic systems are means, not ends. Markets or plans can generate an infinity of outcomes. Choosing a "communist" system, that is a system where the CPC is sovereign, is only a starting point that settles nothing of any real importance. The CPC must comprehensively choose sides.

It has many options. The CPC can decide that the beneficiaries of White Communism are appropriate, and then assess whether their lot can be improved by legalizing freehold property, and expanding the scope of competitive markets.

The CPC can decide that beneficiaries of White Communism are inappropriate, choosing either to reward people in accordance with their value in the competitive market, or some ethical principle like egalitarianism.

If the CPC decides that people should be paid what they competitively earn, then it should abandon White Communism and adopt Liberal Democracy in the most sophisticated sense that allows individual utility seekers to make well-being enhancing adjustments, where utility is a fallible guide.

If the CPC decides that the people cannot competently set public policy, it can uphold the liberal principle in the private sector, but dispense with democracy.

If the CPC decides that it wants to increase the privileges of the rich and powerful, then it should increase the whiteness of White Communism, or switch to a lily-white version of Illiberal Democracy.

If the CPC decides that it wants to privilege victims of injustice and the poor, then it should choose Pink Communism, or switch to Pink Illiberal Democracy.

If the CPC decides that it wants an optimal system with Chinese characteristics that assigns families a critical role in promoting well-being by capturing net external economies, then it should embrace Confucian Liberal Democracy.

These are the CPC's main options. They can be refined by taking account of excluded variables including globalism and populism. White systems may provide higher per capita income than Red systems. Some systems may have better macro-economic and political stability characteristics that deserve consideration.

Ends however are not enough. Systems directors must design and implement incentive mechanisms that are fully compatible with preferred ends. This is very difficult to do, even using a loose satisficing standard, a point that underscores the weakness of all illiberal systems.[215]

The important thing to understand is that no matter how inclusive the analysis, the notion of best in the final analysis must be subjective. "Utiles" and "Well-being-tiles" cannot be quantified and aggregated interpersonally as Jeremy Bentham (1748–1832) mistakenly supposed two centuries ago.[216] The comparative merit of rival economic systems cannot be judged on objective grounds definitively, because no indisputable summary indicator of the "best" exists.

Choosing sides on ethical grounds calls for delicate judgment. The moral worth of Red or White is not a Manichean dichotomy between good and evil, because there is always Pink. The CPC and people everywhere therefore must gather the facts, debate, choose and defend their ethical preferences.[217] A plausible case can be made for the superiority of Compassionate Liberal Democracy, but this too in the final analysis is a matter of taste.

PROSPECTS

Deng Xiaoping's decision to nudge China toward technocratic White Communism in the early 1980s was intuitive. He could not have rationally chosen the best economic system for China because he did not grasp the fundamentals of generally competitive and inclusive economic theory. He initiated Gaige Kaifang because life had taught him that revolutionary Red Communism was a dead end.

Xi Jinping is likely to continue probing the possibilities of China's White Communism in the same way without switching sides by democratizing, reverting to Red Communism or adopting Compassionate Liberal Democracy, Illiberal Democracy or Confucian Liberal Democracy. His path of least resistance is to stay the course unless fate takes a hand.

The improbable could happen. The Soviet Union dissolved itself, and Donald Trump is America's president. If flagging economic development, uneven regional growth, congestion, environmental pollution, a catastrophic financial crisis, a democratic upsurge or Maoist jihadism buffets the CPC, Chinese communism could veer right or left, or be replaced by a non-communist order. Its response will be reactive, but if by some miracle Chinese leaders choose rationally, they should abandon communism. Confucian Liberal Democracy, Compassionate Liberal Democracy and even Illiberal Democracy of various types could all be better choices. Tao Yuanming's Peach Blossom Spring would be a charming choice, but alas, it is only a utopian dream.

NOTES

1 Auslin, *The End of the Asian Century*.
2 Piketty, *Capital in the Twenty-First Century*.
3 Rosefielde, *Trump's Populist America*.
4 Heilbroner, *The Worldly Philosophers*.
5 Becker, *The Economic Approach to Human Behavior*.
6 For example, they may fall under the thrall of "motivated reason". "Motivated reasoning leads people to confirm what they already believe, while ignoring contrary data. But it also drives people to develop elaborate rationalizations to justify holding beliefs that logic and evidence have shown to be wrong. Motivated reasoning responds defensively to contrary evidence, actively discrediting such evidence or its source without logical or evidentiary justification. Clearly, motivated reasoning is emotion driven. It seems to be assumed by social scientists that motivated reasoning is driven by a desire to avoid cognitive dissonance. Self-delusion, in other words, feels good, and that's what motivates people to vehemently defend obvious falsehoods." The Skeptic's Dictionary. http://skepdic.com/motivatedreasoning.html; Lodge and Taber, "Three Steps toward a Theory of Motivated Political Reasoning"; Taber, "The Interpretation of Foreign Policy Events: A Cognitive Process Theory".
7 Kahneman, *Thinking, Fast and Slow*.
8 Leaders may be constrained by institutions, politics and social forces from selecting the path that rationally maximizes well-being. Nelson and Winter, *An Evolutionary Theory of Economic Change*.
9 Chen Duxiu served as General Secretary of the Communist Party from 1921–27. He was expelled from the party in November 1929 for his opposition to the Comintern (Communist International, controlled by Joseph Stalin) and joined Leon Trotsky's Left International Opposition. Li Dazhao's intellectual roots were in Kropotkin's anarchist communism, but he became a Marxist under the influence of the Comintern. He was hanged on April 28, 1927 by the warlord Zhang Zuolin. Both co-founders studied political economy at Waseda University in Japan.
10 Qin Shi Huang, China's first emperor, practiced legalism, a government philosophy tantamount to Mao's and Xi's top-down approach to politics in command.

Confucianism historically is the Chinese governance alternative. It is a bottom-up approach based on self-regulating families cooperating under the guidance of Confucian precepts.

11 https://www.marxists.org/reference/subject/philosophy/help/value.htm

12 Anarchist communism (anarcho-communism) is a theory of stateless communism spontaneously constructed by visionaries with little or no bureaucratic governmental guidance.

13 Engels and Marx, *The Communist Manifesto*, 1848. *Marx's Economic and Philosophical Manuscripts of 1844.* https://www.marxists.org/archive/marx/works/1844/manuscripts/preface.htm

14 The Chinese word laogai, meaning "reform through labor", refers to the most extensive system of forced labor camps in the world – modeled after the Soviet gulag – which has spanned the territory of China since the early days of the communist regime.

15 Rosefielde, *Asian Economic Systems*

16 Ibid.

17 Aristophanes spoofed the fairytale aspect of Marx's adolescent utopia more than 2400 years ago. Somerstein, Alan, Aristophanes's *Ecclesiazusae* (Women in Power Greek), 391 BC.

18 Gérard Debreu won the Nobel Prize in 1983 for proving the existence of a general competitive equilibrium. Debreu, "Existence of competitive equilibrium," 697–744; Debreu, *The Theory of Value: An Axiomatic Analysis of Economic Equilibrium.* The concept of the existence of a general competitive equilibrium using fixed-point mathematical methods was derived among others by Kakutani. The Kakutani fixed-point theorem is for set-valued functions. It provides sufficient conditions for a set-valued function defined on a convex, compact subset of a Euclidean space to have a fixed point, i.e. a point which is mapped to a set containing it. Kakutani "A Generalization of Brouwer's Fixed Point Theorem," 457–9; cf. Nash, "Equilibrium Points in N-Person Games," 48–9.

19 Dorfman, Samuelson, and Solow, *Linear Programming and Economic Analysis.*

20 Rosefielde and Pfouts, *Inclusive Economic Theory.*

21 Gray, *The Socialist Tradition: Moses to Lenin.*

22 Stalin, *Dialectical and Historical Materialism.*

23 Simon, "A behavioral model," 99–118; Simon, *Models of Man: Social and Rational-Mathematical Essays on Rational Human Behavior in a Social Setting*; Simon, "Theories of decision," 99–118; Simon, *Models of Bounded Rationality.*

24 "Legacy of the Great Helmsman," *Economist*, October 16, 1997. http://www.economist.com/node/102928

25 Cf. Rue. *Mao Tse-tung in Opposition, 1927–1935.*

26 During Japan's occupation of China in WWII, the Japanese pillaged, raped, and killed. In rural areas, the wealthy Chinese landlords were the ones who could lose the most from a Japanese occupation; thus many of them became Japanese collaborators. After the war, the People's Liberation Army targeted first the rich Japanese collaborators. Grievance sessions were organized during which poor peasants told the community how they had been previously mistreated by the collaborators. The amount of money or rice that the collaborator owed to the community in compensation was calculated, and payment demanded. When the landlord objected that he did not have the amount demanded, the peasants searched his house. Often, when the basement was opened, piles of rotting grain were discovered. This discovery infuriated the poor peasants because many of them, their friends, neighbors, and relatives had starved (some had even died of starvation) while the landlord let grain rot. Infuriated, the peasants attacked all the major landlords, not just the collaborators (Hinton, William, Fanshen: *A Documentary of Revolution in a Chinese Village* (New York; Vantage Books, 1966), pp 34, 69–79, and 107–134).

The reason landlords let grain rot while their neighbors starved is because China was known for having famines, floods, droughts, and other natural disasters. Even if half of the grain rots away, if the price of the remaining half increases tenfold during a disaster, then the landlord would make huge profits. Letting grain rot while others starve around you is unethical, but it can be the profit maximizing thing to do in a country like China. Mao wanted to eliminate this type of capitalist, counter-revolutionary, attitude.

Angry mobs killed some landlords, other landlords fled, but most landlords stayed and were given small plots of land to farm. When the property of the dispossessed landlords was distributed to the peasants, the peasants received complete private property rights (Meisner, Maurice, *The Deng Xiaoping Era: An Inquiry into the Fate of Chinese Socialism 1978–1994* (New York: Hill and Wang, 1996), p. 28). Because Mao was concerned about disrupting food production excessively, middle income peasants were allowed to keep their lands and even rent some of it out or hire others to work it. Thus the exploitation of labor based on land ownership was not totally eliminated. The land taken from landlords and given to peasants was approximately half of China's farm land (Meisner, Maurice, *Mao's China and After: A History of the People's Republic*, 3rd edition (New York; the Free Press, 1999), p. 90–99).

27 Maurice Meisner (*Mao's China and After: A History of the People's Republic*, 3rd edition (New York; the Free Press, 1999), pp. 71–73) estimates that Mao's repressive measures included 135,000 official executions and 800,000 trials between January and June of 1951. Admitting that his estimate is based on "scanty" information, Meisner's best guess is that there were two million executions in China during the first three years of communist control (including landlords killed by enraged peasant mobs).

28 In the first two years, Mao eliminated China's opium problem (which had existed for two centuries). Furthermore, in the first three years, Mao almost eradicated gambling, alcoholism, and prostitution (Meisner, *Maurice, Mao's China and After: A History of the People's Republic*, 3rd edition (New York; the Free Press, 1999), p. 81–83). Within cities, three early campaigns were run. The thought reform campaign targeted intellectuals. The three-anti movement targeted "corruption, waste, and the bureaucratic spirit." The five anti movement targeted bribery, tax evasion, fraud, and the stealing of government property and state secrets. Like most Maoist campaigns, these combined "struggle sessions" in which participants criticized others and themselves, mass meetings, forced oral and written confessions, and public humiliation (Meisner 1999: 83–87).

There were also material successes. According to Western estimates, China's industrial production increased by 16 percent every year between 1953 and 1957 (Chinese statistics claim 18 percent). Total industrial output produced in China more than doubled between 1953 and 1957. Chinese industries that grew the most between 1952 and 1957 include (Meisner 1999: 113):

1.31 million metric tons of rolled steel grew to 4.48 million metric tons
2.86 million tons of cement grew to 6.86 million tons
1.9 million tons of pig iron grew to 5.9 million tons
66 million tons of coal grew to 130 million tons
7.26 billion kilowatt hours of electricity grew to 19.34 billion kilowatt hours

29 Anarcho-communism is a theory of anarchism which advocates the abolition of the state, capitalism, wage labour and private property (while retaining respect for personal property) and is in favor of common ownership of the means of production, direct democracy and a horizontal network of voluntary associations and workers' councils with production and consumption based on the guiding principle: "from each according to his ability, to each according to his need." Kropotkin, *Mutual Aid: A Factor of*

Evolution; Bakunin, *State and Anarchy*; cf. Marx, *Economic and Philosophical Manuscripts of 1844.*

30 Stalin used the Comintern as a EU-type transnational entity to control non-Soviet communist parties. Mao had the option of placing China entirely under Stalin's wing, but experience taught him better. See Chang and Halliday, *Mao: The Unknown Story.*

31 Neuberger, "Libermanism, Computopia, and Visible Hand," 131–44.

32 State plans were calculated using aggregate production functions, estimates for neutral rates of technological progress and input-output balancing for approximately 100 composite goods.

33 Kantorovich, *The Best Uses of Economic Resources.*

34 Bergson, *The Economics of Soviet Planning.*

35 Rosefielde, *Russian Economy from Lenin to Putin*; for further details, Berliner, *Factory and Manager in the USSR*; Berliner, *The Innovation Decision in Soviet Industry.*

36 The same basic principle applied to revenue and quantity maximizing.

37 Mao's long term plan was to collectivize China's farm land after China was industrialized, a plan that put collectivization twenty plus years in the future. His plan also entailed collectivize the land voluntarily. He intended to show the peasants that collectivization would increase productivity, increasing everyone's wealth, resulting in an enthusiastic, voluntary collectivization. However, Mao decided that waiting for the productivity gains from collectivization was not a viable option after the weaker-than-hoped-for harvests of 1953–1957. Mao launched a collectivization of farm land drive on July 31, 1955 (Meisner, Maurice, *Mao's China and After: A History of the People's Republic*, 3rd edition (New York; the Free Press, 1999), p. 129–137). In December of 1954 only two percent of farming households were in cooperatives, by December of 1956 this number had surged to 98 percent (Naughton, Barry, *The Chinese Economy: Transitions and Growth* (Cambridge, Massachusetts, MIT Press, 2007), p. 67). Meisner 1999, chapter 9 provides more details. Collectivization only took two years because when local government officials heard Mao's plan, they wanted to be the first to implement it in order to receive Mao's praise and a possible promotion and they feared being the last to implement it because they did not want to be labeled a "counter-revolutionary."

Collectivization produced neither the surges of agricultural production that Mao had hoped for, nor the disaster that opponents had predicted. On the positive side, collectives mobilized large numbers of peasants for the improvement of agricultural infrastructure, like the digging of hundreds of miles of irrigation ditches, which would not have happened under relatively small individually owned farms. Furthermore, collectives provided peasants with improved educational opportunities, health care, and security (Meisner 1999: 147–148).

38 In 1960 Mao lost control of the Chinese Communist Party due to the failures of the Great Leap Forward and widespread famine (Meisner, *Maurice, Mao's China and After: A History of the People's Republic*, 3rd edition (New York; the Free Press, 1999), pp. 250–254). In many ways, the ideas underlying the Great Leap Forward were rational. China's terrain, weather, and altitude make her poorly suited for agriculture. In 1949, China had lots of labor, very little capital, and relatively little excellent land for cultivation. Heckscher-Ohlin theory would advise China to develop the production of labor intensive goods. Contrary to this theory, the First Five Year Plan emphasized capital intensive heavy industry. In contrast, the Great Leap Forward aimed to develop labor intensive light industry also. China was to walk on two feet – heavy industry and light industry together (Meisner 1999: 206–209). Furthermore, locating light industry in rural areas where the majority of Chinese lived made sense. Moreover, agricultural production results in large blocks of slack time, which could be used for labor intensive production.

Also light industry located in rural areas should reduce rural to urban migration and increase employment. (Meisner 1999: 204–209).

During the Great Leap Forward, Mao encouraged the transformation of agricultural collectives into communes. By December 1958, approximately 750,000 collective farms had been merged and re-organized into 24,000 communes. The average commune contained 5,000 households. However, these communes varied noticeably in size from some incorporating less than 5,000 people and others more than 100,000 people (Meisner 1999: 210–212 and 214–220).

The large size of communes made huge projects possible, like digging hundreds of miles of irrigation trenches. While men worked on big projects, women worked in the fields. Elderly women cared for children and cooked in communal halls. According to Mao "women uphold half of heaven" and they deserved the responsibilities and status that came from doing so. The approximately 7% of cultivated land that remained as the "private property" of individual households at the beginning of 1958 was almost entirely eliminated by the end of that year (Meisner 1999: 221–223).

Some Great Leap Forward projects were successes like the production of pesticides, fertilizer, and some consumer goods, the repair and manufacturing of farm equipment, and the small scale generation of electricity and refining of oil. One of the biggest failures was "backyard" steel mills. The homemade steel furnaces made by peasants did not get hot enough to burn out impurities which resulted in many household metal tools, like frying pans, being melted down into brittle, useless metal (Meisner 1999: 224 and 231).

Food shortages of the fall of 1958 diminished peasant support of the communes. On November 28, 1958 the communist party (as encouraged by Liu Shaoqi) returned to the approach used in the former collectives by defining the "production brigade" as the major production unit, restoring the small "private" plots of land previously used by individual families to grow additional food, and re-centralizing control of agriculture under the national communist party. Mao objected. By mid-1959, most communal mess halls had shut down, markets had reemerged in rural areas, and peasants were spending more and more time working their "private" family plots of land (Meisner 1999: 228–230).

Initially an estimated 375,000,000 tons of grain was produced in 1958; however, this figure was later revised to 250,000,000 tons. In contrast, Meisner (1999: 233) believes that 1958's grain production was only 215,000,000 tons. In 1959, grain production fell to only 170,000,000 tons (Meisner 1999: 236). However, the central government's grain tax was based upon the amount of grain local government officials reported which was exaggerated. As grain production plummeted in 1959, the amount of grain taken by the central government increased. In 1960, droughts dried up the lower two thirds of the Yellow River, the South was flooded by typhoons, and insects devastated even more of the crops. Consequentially, 1960's grain production fell to 144,000,000 tons. Some experts believe that 15 million died from these problems (Meisner 1999: 234–238) and others argue that there were 25 to 30 million excess deaths (Naughton, Barry, *The Chinese Economy: Transitions and Growth* (Cambridge, Massachusetts, MIT Press, 2007), p. 71–72).

Relative to its 1958–1959 levels, 1962's industrial production was down by almost 40 percent. The shutting down of thousands of small, inefficient factories and a freeze on hiring caused China's industrial work force to fall to half of its previous level. Unemployed workers in the cities were sent to rural areas to become farmers (Meisner 1999: 264). After the famine of 1960, China's government augmented the anti-Marxist policies of November 1958. For communist cadres, pay differentials based on thirty ranks were introduced. Bonuses were used to spur increased productivity from workers and peasants. "Profitability" was emphasized and "petty capitalism" openly allowed. More and more firms turned to paying individual workers by the number of pieces they personally produced (Meisner 1999: 251–253).

"Private" farm plots and markets expanded. Although the central government limited private plots to no more than six percent of cultivatable land, Meisner believes that the actual percent used as private plots exceeded twelve percent. By the mid-1960s, almost one-third of peasant income came from their private plots. Liu Shaoqi, who now controlled the communist party, replaced hundreds of thousands of pro-Mao rural cadres with pro-communist party cadres. The communist party went so far as to denounce "egalitarianism," and to subdivide the 24,000 communes into 74,000 smaller units (Meisner 1999: 261–263). Great Leap Forward pro-equality policies to spread education and medicine to rural areas were ended (Meisner 1999: 266–267).

In the 1962–1965 Socialist Education Movement, Mao tried to fight back against this abandoning of Marxist ideals. Mao tried to use this movement to restore collectivism and communes and to "cleanse" elitism and corruption from the Communist Party. Mao's May 1963 resolution, "First Ten Points," included a call for cadres to work in the fields with the peasants. Liu Shaoqi and Deng Xiaoping countered by issuing the "Later Ten Points" and the "Revised Later Ten Points" which blunted the radical Marxist nature of Mao's movement. In a move that would increase his personal power, Mao encouraged a personality cult that practically deified himself (Meisner 1999: 273–281).

39 China's "century of humiliation" was ended by the Korean War (Meisner, Maurice, *Mao's China and After: A History of the People's Republic*, 3rd edition (New York; the Free Press, 1999), pp. 69–71). In the early 1800s, China was exporting more to the British Empire than the Empire was exporting to China. As a result China acquired British silver. Wanting to reverse the flow of silver, the British suggested that the Chinese government legalize the use of opium (which was produced in the British colony of India) and tax it. The Chinese rejected this British suggestion and tried to stop the smuggling of opium into China by seizing a British ship carrying opium near China's coast. The British Empire attacked China to force China to pay for the destroyed opium shipment and to allow the future importation of opium. The morality of this war is even more questionable when one realizes that opium was illegal in Brittan at the time. Upon winning the war, Britain took Hong Kong away from China (but gave it back in 1997) and forced China to open five ports to British trade (Naughton, Barry, *The Chinese Economy: Transitions and Growth* (Cambridge, Massachusetts, MIT Press, 2007), p. 40–42). China had at least eleven major international conflicts in the hundred years between the first opium War and the Korean War, losing every one of them. China fighting the world's most powerful military, the USA's, to a bloody stand still in the Korean War ended China's losing streak and gave Mao tremendous internal prestige in the process (Meisner 1999: 69–71).

40 Mao wanted to abandon the Soviet model; the Central Committee did not agree. In response, Mao reviving the saying, "let a hundred flowers blossom, let a hundred schools of thought contend" which encouraged intellectuals to freely criticize the party. Warning that "poisonous weeds" would spring up with the flowers, the communist party opposed the "contending and blooming." Initially the intellectuals did not answer Mao's call because they feared criticizing the government (Meisner, Maurice, *Mao's China and After: A History of the People's Republic*, 3rd edition (New York; the Free Press, 1999), pp. 149–150 and 155–174). In the middle of 1957, China's intellectuals finally embraced Mao's permission to criticize the party. Their criticisms included the Communist Party's monopoly on power being inconsistent with Marxian and socialist thought. China's intellectuals accused the Communist Party of having become a privileged class that was

enriching itself at the expense of the general population, just as the Kuomintang and mandarins had done (Meisner 1999: 174–180).

An editorial in the *People's Daily* on June 8, 1957 removed the permission to criticize the government that was given in the Hundred Flowers Campaign. Some of the intellectuals who had criticized the government were publically condemned, forced to confess their crimes, and/or were subjected to "labor reform" in an "Anti-rightist Campaign." Mao used this "Anti-rightist" campaign to purge the communist leadership of those that opposed him. By 1958, this purge involved the reprimanding, expulsion, or probation of a million party members. This purge resulted in Mao regaining control of China's leadership (Meisner 1999: 180–188).

41 For the first five year plan, Mao embraced the Soviet model which made a single leader responsible for his or her factory. Mao allowed each worker to be rewarded based on how much he or she produced, his or her skill, and his or her expertise. This approach increased wage differentials. For leaders, there were 26 ranks associated with monthly salaries between 30 yuan and 560 yuan, US$ 12 to US$ 224, (Meisner, Maurice, Mao's China and After: A History of the People's Republic, 3rd edition (New York; the Free Press, 1999), pp. 108–119).

42 In 1960, Wu Han wrote a play entitled *Hai Rui Dismissed from Office* about a corrupt Ming dynasty emperor who destroyed a local virtuous government official who had protested the taking of peasant lands by greedy landlords and corrupt officials.

In November 1965, Yao Wenyuan (a minor literary critic who later became one of the "Gang of Four") critiqued the play because the evil emperor represented Mao Zedong and the taking of peasant lands referred to the setting up of the communes during the Great Leap Forward to which Peng Dehuai, the virtuous local official, had objected and for which he was sacked.

Mao called for a mobilization of the people to cleanse the Communist Party of capitalist saboteurs at all levels, including the top (specifically Liu Shaoqi and Deng Xiaoping). University and middle school students responded to this call and formed groups of "Red Guards." On May 25, 1966, the students of Beijing University (with the encouragement of a young philosophy instructor, Nie Yuanzi) put up a "big-character poster" condemning the president of the University for suppressing campus discussions of the Wu Han situation. Party authorities tore down the poster and punished those involved. A week later, Mao praised the poster and the courage of those who put it up.

In June 1966, Liu Shaoqi sent party teams to campuses to organize and give party guidance to the Red Guard groups. The groups organized by the party often were led by the sons and daughters of party officials. In contrast the groups that responded to Mao's initial call often included those who had the greatest grievances against the Communist Party – the sons and daughters of the disposed landlords. Both the "party-organized" and the "self-organized" Red Guards swore allegiance to Mao and quoted him extensively. However, the self-organized Red Guards attacked party officials, while the party-organized Red Guards attacked "bourgeois elements" meaning intellectuals, professors and writers. Their targets were often paraded around town, wearing dunce caps, and forced to confess their crimes. In late July, Mao ordered the party-sponsored work teams to leave the schools and condemned the previous "fifty days of White Terror." Mao insisted that the party not interfere in the forming of Red Guard groups since the party was the major target.

On August 18, 1966 a million young Chinese crowded into Tiananmen Square to see Mao appear above the Gate of Heavenly Peace at sunrise to don a Red Guard armband, proclaim himself the "Supreme Commander" of the Red Guards and give them his blessing. In addition to attacking the Communist Party, the Red Guards attacked the "four olds": old customs, old culture, old habits and old ideas. This campaign resulted in the destruction of museums and places of worship for Taoism, Buddhism, Confucianism and Christianity. Many books and works of art were burned. The self-organized and the party-organized Red Guards also fought each other. The People's Liberation Army was instructed to help the Red Guards, who were given food and shelter wherever they went and were allowed to use railroads, trucks and buses for free. Mao held eight Red Guard rallies in Tiananmen Square to which a total of twelve million Red Guards came.

By the fall of 1966, the Cultural Revolution in Shanghai had spread from schools to factories. Again there emerged major differences between the groups organized by those who benefited from the past communist leadership (skilled workers with lifetime employment and bonuses) and those who did not (the unemployed and contract workers with no job security and minimal pay). An alliance of groups hurt by the current system emerged named the "Headquarters of the Revolutionary Revolt of Shanghai Workers" led by Wang Hongwen (a textile worker who later became one of the Gang of Four). On November 8, 1966 the Headquarters demanded that the Communist Party of Shanghai recognize the Headquarters as the legitimate government of Shanghai and give an accounting of its past administration. After an initial delay, Beijing backed up the Headquarters which led to the rapid disintegration of Shanghai's party apparatus. Opposing the Headquarters was the "Workers' Scarlet Guards for the Defense of Mao Zedong Thought," which consisted primarily of skilled workers and technicians. Fighting between the two groups ensued, a general strike was called, and a previous Shanghai party leader, Zhang Chunqiao, tried to take control of the revolution by forming an alliance with Wang Hongwen of the Headquarters and by using the army and police to suppress dissent.

Mao intervened by calling Wang Hongwen and Zhang Chunqiao to Beijing where he told them to give up the idea of forming a "commune" and instead form a "revolutionary committee." Revolutionary committees consisted of an alliance between revolutionary organizations, the Party, and the army where the army was in control. In some places there was armed resistance to this betrayal of the ideals of the Cultural Revolution, and in the city of Wuhan troops, tanks, three infantry divisions, navy gunboats and an airborne unit got involved. In many places, the revolutionaries attacked the army, accusing it of "bourgeois" inclinations. Mao went on a provincial inspection tour, and then (on September 5, 1967) commanded the army to restore order, period. In spite of the masses being told to cooperate with the army, hundreds of thousands of people were killed as the army reestablished control. The students were told to return to their studies; however, between 1967 and 1976, 17,000,000 urban youth were sent to the countryside to learn from hard work and the peasants, which conveniently scattered them and put them where they could do little damage.

43   Wheelwright and McFarlane, *The Chinese Road to Socialism: Economics of the Cultural Revolution*; Rosefielde, *World Communism at the Crossroads: Military Ascendancy, Political Economy and Human Welfare*, 260–73.

44   Communist and Confucian self-regulation rely on popular initiative, but differ in philosophy. Confucians are guided by elaborate moral precepts. The Red Guard adhered to liberationist dogma with little coherence ethical content.

45   It was so opaque that two different groups of red guards emerged that fought each other. One group aimed at overthrowing corrupt leaders in the communist party; the other group aimed at overthrowing bourgeois intellectuals in society.

46   In 1960, Wu Han wrote the play "*Hai Jui Dismissed from Office.*" In the play an evil Ming dynasty emperor destroyed an ethical rural government official after he protested when corrupt government officials and greedy landlords took land from peasants. In November 1965, Yao Wenyuan (who ultimately became one of the "Gang of Four,"

but at this time was a minor literary critic) argued that the evil emperor represented Mao who took the land of peasants when he set up the communes. The virtuous rural government official represented Peng Dehuai, who was fired for objecting to the setting up of the communes.

In May 1966, Nie Yuanzi, a philosophy professor, encouraged Beijing University students to create and display a "big-character poster" criticizing the President of Beijing University for prohibiting campus discussions of Wu Han's play and Yao Wenyuan's critique of it. Communist authorities removed the poster and punished the people involved. Mao, a week later, praised the courage of the students and the poster. Around this time, Mao issued a call to the people of China for them to rise up and cleanse the government of capitalist saboteurs who had infiltrated all levels of the government from the top (i.e. Liu Shaoqi and Deng Xiaoping) to the bottom. In answer to this call, middle school and especially university students formed groups of "Red Guards."

In June 1966, Liu Shaoqi sent teams, loyal to the communist party, to campuses for the purpose of organizing and giving party guidance to groups of Red Guards. These teams set up Red Guard groups led by the sons and daughters of communist party officials. In contrast, many of the Red Guard groups formed in response to Mao's initial call included the sons and daughters of the disposed landlords – i.e. those with the greatest grievances against China's Communist Party. Both "party-organized" and "self-organized" Red Guard groups quoted Mao and swore allegiance to him. The party organized Red Guards attacked professors, writers, and intellectuals, calling them "bourgeois elements." The self-organized Red Guards attacked communist party officials. Both sets of targets were forced to confess their crimes, wear dunce caps, and were often paraded around town in a humiliating fashion. In July 1966, Mao publically condemned the "Fifty Days of White Terror" caused by the communist party organized Red Guards and commanded that the party stop interfering in the Red Guard movement, because the party was the primary target.

On August 18, 1966 a million Red Guards crowded into Tiananmen Square where Mao appear at sunrise above the Gate of Heavenly Peace and donned a Red Guard armband. Mao proclaim that he was the "Supreme Commander" of all Red Guards, and Mao blessed them. The Red Guards also attacked the "four olds:" old customs, old culture, old habits, and old ideas, which resulted in destruction of places of worship and museums. Works of art and books were burned. The party-organized and self-organized Red Guards fought each other. The People's Liberation Army was commanded to help Red Guards by allowing them to use railways, trucks and buses for free and by giving them food and shelter.

By the autumn of 1966 in Shanghai, the Cultural Revolution had spread from school campuses to factories. Again, two major groups were formed: (1) skilled workers, who earned bonuses and enjoyed life time employment, tended to coalesce into groups that had benefited from previous communist leadership and (2) contract workers and the unemployed coalesce into groups who felt betrayed by the communist party. Wang Hongwen (who later became one of the Gang of Four, but now was a mere textile worker) formed an alliance of groups with grievances against the communist party and named it the "Headquarters of the Revolutionary Revolt of Shanghai Workers." On November 8, 1966 the "Headquarters" proclaimed itself the legitimate government of Shanghai and demanded that the past Communist Party led government of Shanghai submit an accounting of its administration. When Beijing finally responded, she supported the Headquarters, causing a rapid deterioration of Shanghai's communist party apparatus. The "Workers' Scarlet Guards for the Defense of Mao Zedong Thought" opposed the Headquarters. The two groups fought, a general strike was called, and

Zhang Chunqiao tried to take control by forming an alliance with Wang Hongwen and by using the police and army to stop open dissent. Zhang's goal was to change Shanghai into a commune.

Mao summoned Wang Hongwen and Zhang Chunqiao to Beijing and told them to form a "revolutionary committee," not a commune. Revolutionary committees were to be controlled by the Army in consultation with revolutionary organizations and the communist party. Many saw these revolutionary committees as a betrayal of the ideals of the Cultural Revolution, and fighting ensued. In Wuhan tanks, three infantry divisions, an airborne unit, and navy gunboats were used to suppress displeasure with the shift to revolutionary committees. On September 5, 1967, Mao commanded the armed forces to use whatever force was needed to restore order. Hundreds of thousands of Chinese citizens were killed by the army as it reestablished control. A blanket command was issued to all students to return to their studies. However, by 1976, a total of 17,000,000 urban youth had been rounded up and sent to rural areas to learn from peasants and hard work.

If the Cultural Revolution is viewed as a contest between Mao and his political opponents, then Mao won. After the revolution, Mao's Great Leap Forward rural policies were re-introduced, which had been opposed by Liu Shaoqi. Liu had allowed private farming plots to grown to 15 percent of cultivable land; Mao now imposed a 5 percent limit. Liu had freed rural markets; Mao tried to minimize them. Liu emphasized industrialization in cities; Mao built industries in the country side. By 1976 (when Mao died) rural areas produced fifty percent of China's chemical fertilizer, a large percent of the nation's farm machinery, and a substantial amount of construction materials, pharmaceuticals, electricity, and chemicals. By Mao's death, rural industry employed 20,000,000 peasants on a full time or part time basis.

When Liu was in control, the number of urban health clinics doubled and 71 percent of rural clinics were closed. After the Cultural Revolution, Mao required all urban medical staff to serve in rural areas on a rotating basis. Before his death in 1976, Mao sent out a million bare foot doctors primarily to rural areas, representing a fourfold increase since 1965. Mao also reallocated education funds from urban areas to rural areas. Between 1966 and 1967, rural primary school enrollment increased to 150 million from 116 million, meanwhile rural secondary school enrollments increased to 58 million from 15 million. In contrast, by the mid-1970s, university enrollments in the cities were only one-third of what they had been pre-Cultural Revolution.

All of the above information on the Great Cultural Revolution comes from Meisner, Maurice, *Mao's China and After: A History of the People's Republic*, 3rd edition (New York; the Free Press, 1999), pp. 312, 315–323, 326–345, and 352–369.

47 Rosefielde and Latane, "Decentralized Economic Control in the Soviet Union and Maoist China", 260–73.

48 Yugoslavia (1918–2006) established a worker-managed, Communist Party–managed economic system. Horvat, Marcovic and Supek eds., *Self-Governing Socialism*.

49 Revolutionary committees were tripartite bodies established during China's Cultural Revolution to facilitate government by three mass organizations – the people, the PLA and the Party. They were originally established as a replacement system of government to the old Party apparatus, but quickly became subordinate to it. See MacFarquhar and Schoenhals, *Mao's Last Revolution*.

50 Coase, "The Problem of Social Cost," 1–44.

51 Mao emerged from the Cultural Revolution victorious, revered as a demi-god. He resumed his advocacy of Great Leap Forward rural policies, limiting private plots

and repressing free rural markets. He championed rural industrialization, created a million "barefoot" doctors to service rural areas and promoted non-urban education.

By the time the Great Helmsman died, local rural industries were producing one-half of China's chemical fertilizer, as well as a large percentage of China's farm machinery. Rural areas also produced construction materials (including cement and pig iron), electricity, pharmaceuticals and chemicals. By 1976, 20,000,000 peasants were employed on a full-time or part-time basis in industry.

In spite of advances in rural health and education, the aftermath of the Cultural Revolution did not fundamentally change the fact that urban areas provided much better pay and opportunities than the rural areas provided. However, the urban working class received fewer additional benefits from the Cultural Revolution than the rural areas did. Weak efforts were made to address the urban proletariat's complaints about inequality, the exploitation of temporary workers and piecemeal pay, and constraints on the freedom of workers to change employers. However, these efforts were short-lived and produced no fundamental changes. For example, although the use of temporary and contract pay had been severely condemned as a particularly evil form of capitalist exploitation during the Cultural Revolution, those systems were not changed afterwards – almost half of the non-agricultural labor force continued to be exploited by these capitalist institutions.

Likewise pay inequalities were similar before and after the Cultural Revolution. For example, at one Beijing factory the average pay for cadres, engineers and technicians was 150 yuan per month, in contrast to the average worker's pay of 54 yuan per month (the national eight-level pay system for workers ranged from 30 to 108 yuan/month). Temporary and contract workers usually received less than 30 yuan per month. Communist Party cadres continued to be paid according to a 24-tiered system and to enjoy free meals and expenses while on duty. The highest ranking officials were provided with houses, servants, cars, chauffeurs and vacations.

52 Rosefielde, *Red Holocaust*.

53 "Iron rice bowl" is a Chinese term used to refer to an occupation with guaranteed job security, as well as steady income and benefits. Hughes, *China's Economic Challenge*.

54 Sommerstein, *Aristophanes' Ecclesiazusae*. This play, written in 391 BC, is about a communist utopia established by women in their husbands' absence. The women, led by Praxagora, institute a communist-like government in which the state feeds, houses and generally takes care of every Athenian. They enforce equality by allowing each man to sleep with any woman, provided that he first sleeps with every woman in Athens who is uglier than the woman he wants. Private property is abolished and all money and property are to go into a common fund. All expenses and purchases by each individual are to come out of the common fund. Any individual with personal property is considered to have stolen from the community.

55 Tao Yuanming (365–427), also known as Tao Qian or T'ao Ch'ien, was a Chinese poet who lived in the middle of the Six Dynasties period (c. 220–589 CE). *Peach Blossom Spring Story*, or *The Peach Blossom Land*, was a fable by Tao Yuanming in 421 about a chance discovery of an ethereal utopia where the people lead an ideal existence in harmony with nature, unaware of the outside world for centuries.

56 Literati, scholars in China and Japan whose poetry, calligraphy and paintings were supposed primarily to reveal their cultivation and express their personal feelings rather than demonstrate professional skill. The concept of literati painters was first formulated in China in the Bei (Northern) Song dynasty but was enduringly codified in the Ming

dynasty by Dong Qichang. Swartz, *Reading Tao Yuanming: Shifting Paradigms of Historical Reception (427–1900)*.

57 When Mao died, three groups vied for control: Hua Guofeng, Deng Xiaoping, and the Gang of Four. Hua was officially in control, and he arranged for the simultaneous arrest of each member of the Gang of Four and repeatedly denounced Deng Xiaoping. The Gang of Four consisted of people who had played major roles in the Cultural Revolution — Jiang Qing (Mao's widow), Zhang Chunqiao, Wang Hongwen, and Yao Wenyuan (Meisner, Maurice, *The Deng Xiaoping Era: An Inquiry into the Fate of Chinese Socialism 1978–1994* (New York: Hill and Wang, 1996), p. 61–70 and Vogel, Ezra F., *Deng Xiaoping: and the Transformation of China* (Cambridge, Massachusetts: Harvard University Press, 2011), p. 172–181). Hua promised to do "whatever" Mao would have done (Vogel 2011: 188).

Hua's administration tried to re-start higher education, announced a new "hundred flowers" policy, and attempted the "Four Modernizations." The four areas targeted for modernized were defense, industry, agriculture, and science and technology. The goal was for China to be a "powerful, modern socialist country" by the year 2000. To further that goal, Hua planned to import modern technology, give complete managerial control to factories, and increase material rewards for workers. Specific actions taken by the Hua administration included (1) establishing the first special economic zones and (2) giving of a ten percent raise to most state owned enterprise laborers, government workers, and teachers — the first raise in more than two decades (Meisner 1996: 71–74).

58 More than two years late (in February 1978), Hua Guofeng announced China's development plan for 1976–1985. In this plan, Hua proposed more capital construction for 1978 to 1985 (eight years) than the total construction of capital between 1949 and 1977 (twenty eight years). Hua's plan included a doubling of steel and coal production and assumed that mechanizing 85 percent of farms by 1985 would double agriculture's average annual growth rate (Meisner, Maurice, *The Deng Xiaoping Era: An Inquiry into the Fate of Chinese Socialism 1978–1994* (New York: Hill and Wang, 1996), p. 78–79). In order to pay for massive amounts of foreign capital and technology, Hua said China would export the oil found in new (not yet discovered) oil fields, and export agricultural surpluses. According to China's official planners in 1978, Hua's plan would require an estimated fourteen times the money invested between 1949 to 1959 (Meisner 1996: 78–80). It soon became obvious that there was no way to adequately fund Hua's plan. Like other Chinese leaders, Hua Guofeng's power and control ebbed when his keynote policies failed (Meisner, Maurice, *Mao's China and After: A History of the People's Republic*, 3rd edition (New York; the Free Press, 1999), p. 430).

59 The Chinese Communist Party classifies Deng Xiaoping today as a "core" leader together with Mao Zedong, Jiang Zemin, and Xi Jinping. But Deng's position just before Mao's death in 1976 was precarious. Zhou Enlai, a natural peace maker, was China's Premier under Mao Zedong. Zhou was widely loved and respected by the Chinese and foreigners. Zhou openly wanted Deng Xiaoping to become the next Premier (Meisner, Maurice, *Mao's China and After: A History of the People's Republic*, 3rd edition (New York; the Free Press, 1999), p. 403). Unfortunately for Deng, Zhou Enlai died (January 8, 1976) before Mao (September 9, 1976). Upon Zhou's death, Mao made Hua Guofeng, the Minister of Public Security, the acting Premier. Mao did not go to Zhou's funeral where Deng gave the eulogy (Vogel, Ezra F., *Deng Xiaoping: and the Transformation of China* (Cambridge, Massachusetts: Harvard University Press, 2011), p. 158). On January 11, 1976 in freezing weather, between one to two million Chinese lined the street to see Zhou's funeral procession. By January 12th, approximately

two million people had brought wreaths and eulogies in honor of Zhou to Tiananmen Square (Vogel 2011: 159).

   In direct defiance of the Chinese government's condemnation of the Qing Ming festival (which honors the dead) and her forbidding the placing wreaths in Tiananmen Square, a massive number of Chinese (some estimate two million) filled Tiananmen Square with wreaths, poems, wall posters, and eulogies honoring Zhou the day before Qing Ming (April 4, 1976). That night, the government had the wreaths removed. On Qing Ming, angry Chinese, by the tens of thousands, marched to the square and protested that their tributes to Zhou had been prematurely eliminated. The Chinese Communist Party declared the wreaths and protests a "counterrevolutionary incident" and claimed that Deng Xiaoping had orchestrated it. Later this incident was named the "April Fifth Movement." As punishment, Deng was fired (stripped of all his official posts). Deng was accused of being "an unrepentant capitalist-roader" and his modernization plans labeled "the three poisonous weeds." Having eliminated the Gang of Four and Deng Xiaoping, Hua Goufeng was confirmed as Premier (Meisner 1999: 403–4 and Vogel 2011: 165–170).

60 Nolan, "The China Puzzle," 25. There was an important neoclassical precedent for this hypothesis. See Lange, "On the Economic Theory of Socialism I," 53–71.

61 Deng's policy that "Practice is the Sole Criteria for Truth" struggled against Hua's policy of "Whatever Mao would have done." Politicians who gained power in the Cultural Revolution tended to support Hua Goufeng's leadership while Deng Xiaoping attracted people who the Cultural Revolution had hurt. Deng supported freedom of the press and democracy as long as the press was critical of Hua (but when the press criticized Deng's attack on Vietnam, Deng turned against the press). Deng's speeches and policies often implicitly criticized Mao, but no one dared to explicitly criticize Mao. On July 17, 1977, Hua gave into pressure and rehired Deng giving him the rank of third from the top. Deng volunteered to oversee China's efforts in education, science, and technology. Deng strongly promoted a meritocratic elite based on training and ability, not class background. In 1977, Deng re-introduce university entrance exams. In 1978, Deng encouraged Chinese scientists to have contact with Western scientists; overthrowing a 1950 policy that prohibited such contacts (Vogel, Ezra F., *Deng Xiaoping: and the Transformation of China* (Cambridge, Massachusetts: Harvard University Press, 2011), p. 180–265, 321, and 349–373).

   By 1978, Hua had less real power than Deng. By 1980, there was no question — Deng had become the top leader. After June 1981, Hua rarely attended even important meetings (Vogel 2011: 180–265, 349–373, 377 and Meisner, Maurice, *The Deng Xiaoping Era: An Inquiry into the Fate of Chinese Socialism 1978–1994* (New York: Hill and Wang, 1996), pp. 63–136, 434).

62 On March 30, 1979 in the "Four Cardinal Principles," Deng prohibited criticisms of (1) the socialist path, (2) the dictatorship of the proletariat, (3) the leadership of the Communist Party, and (4) Marxism-Leninism and Mao Zedong Thought. Deng ended his "State of China" speech of January 16, 1980 with, "Without party leadership, it would be impossible to achieve anything in contemporary China" (Vogel, Ezra F., *Deng Xiaoping: and the Transformation of China* (Cambridge, Massachusetts: Harvard University Press, 2011), p. 362 and 423). Deng's revision of China's constitution eliminated the "Four Great Freedoms" – the freedoms to speak out freely, to air views fully, to hold great debates, and to write big-character banners (Vogel 2011: 362).

63 When Marx's "end of history" arrives, markets still will be useful for realizing Marx's need-based communist dream in an advanced complex modern setting.

64 Deng knew that some other Chinese communist leaders would oppose the controversial policies he wanted implemented. Therefore Deng would advocate testing these policies in limited areas of China first. If objections were raised, Deng would argue that they were just experimenting and that if the experiment did not work then it would not be implemented elsewhere. For example, Deng first experimented with the household responsibility system in Anhui province, where massive starvation and poverty were severe (Vogel, Ezra F., *Deng Xiaoping: and the Transformation of China* (Cambridge, Massachusetts: Harvard University Press, 2011), pp. 390 and 435–445). When other leaders objected, a supporter of Deng, Wan Li, yelled, "You have a fat head and big ears [you are like a pig]. You have plenty to eat. The peasants are thin because they do not have enough to eat. How can you tell the peasants they can't find a way to have enough to eat?" (interview with Yao Jianfu, who attended the meeting, April 2009 as reported in Vogel 2011: 439). Likewise the first four Special Economic Zones (SEZ) were just "experiments."

However, Deng wanted his experiments to work, so he gave them advantages that could not be given across all of China. For example, Deng arranged for the infrastructure of the experimental SEZs to be built and gave these SEZs huge tax breaks (Meisner, Maurice, *The Deng Xiaoping Era: An Inquiry into the Fate of Chinese Socialism 1978–1994* (New York: Hill and Wang, 1996), p. 274–283 and Vogel 2011: 402). Deng also personally investigated allegations of problems in the experiments and then proclaim the experiments a success. Deng was daring anyone to express contrary views since Deng himself had personally investigated.

65 Markets could be beneficially employed under full communism to facilitate transactions that cannot be consummated effectively on a face-to-face basis.

66 Except in the military–industrial complex and affiliated sectors.

67 Guaranteed state purchase and subsidies are abolished.

68 The ultimate freehold owner is the state. Private shareholders lease usage rights from the state.

69 Locke, *Second Treatise on Government*. This is called the rule of law.

70 In September 1980, the Party Central Committee endorsed the "production responsibility system," which allowed rural households to form contracts with their local production team allowing the household to privately farm a specific part of land in exchange for an agreed upon percent of the resulting output. The former collective's tools and animals were allocated to specific households to use in their private farming. William Hinton ((1989), "A Response to Hugh Deane," *Monthly Review*, 40(10), p. 20–21 as cited in Meisner, Maurice, *The Deng Xiaoping Era: An Inquiry into the Fate of Chinese Socialism 1978–1994* (New York: Hill and Wang, 1996), p. 245–246) see also Meisner, Maurice, *Mao's China and After: A History of the People's Republic*, 3rd edition (New York; the Free Press, 1999), p. 476) described this distribution of farm equipment and machinery as follows.

When the time came to distribute collective assets, people with influence and connections – cadres, their relatives, friends, and cronies – were able to buy, at massive discounts, the tractors, trucks, wells, pumps, processing equipment, and other productive property that the collectives had accumulated over decades through the hard labor of all members. Not only did the buyers manage to set low prices for these capital assets (often one-third or less of their true value), but they often bought them with easy credit from state banks and then, in the end, often failed to pay what they had promised.

By December 1983, the production responsibility system had spread to ninety eight percent of all farming households (Meisner 1996: 227–229).

71 Pragmatism is a philosophy that claims that ideas and ideologies that don't generate practical results should be rejected, even if they are logically consistent. Conversely,

concepts that yield practical results should be accepted, even if they are incomplete. The attitude is the obverse of utopianism. The concept was formally developed in the nineteenth century by Charles Sanders Peirce, and popularized later by William James and John Dewey. It was influential in Chinese pedagogical circles, despite its *bourgeois* pedigree.

72 Although Mao initiated Town and Village enterprises (TVEs) in the Communes during the Great Leap Forward, TVEs did not achieve their apex until the Deng era. Most TVEs produced services and goods using abundant labor and low technology. On average, rural industrial output increased by 37.7 percent per year between 1984 and 1987. TVE employment of 28.3 million people in 1978 grew to 105.8 million in 1992 and then to 135 million by 1996. In 1978 commune industry produced 49 billion yuan of value which grew to 1798 billion yuan by 1992. In 1978 nine percent of China's total industrial output was produced in commune industries; but this percent grew to 25 percent in 1990 and then to 42 percent in 1994. Many western economists are bothered by TVEs because they were both communally owned and very successful (Meisner, Maurice, *The Deng Xiaoping Era: An Inquiry into the Fate of Chinese Socialism 1978–1994* (New York: Hill and Wang, 1996), p. 231–232; Vogel, Ezra F., *Deng Xiaoping: and the Transformation of China* (Cambridge, Massachusetts: Harvard University Press, 2011), pp. 445–447; and Naughton, Barry, *The Chinese Economy: Transitions and Growth* (Cambridge, Massachusetts, MIT Press, 2007), pp. 271–293).

73 In 1983 and 1984 China's communist government passed new laws which allowed rural wage laborers to be hired and contracted land to be rented (Meisner, Maurice, *The Deng Xiaoping Era: An Inquiry into the Fate of Chinese Socialism* 1978–1994 (New York: Hill and Wang, 1996), p. 230). In 1984, land contracts were limited to no more than fifteen years; however, the maximum temporal length of land contracts was soon increased to thirty years (Meisner 1996: 230 and Naughton, Barry, *The Chinese Economy: Transitions and Growth* (Cambridge, Massachusetts, MIT Press, 2007), p. 241). Both Naughton and Meisner and Naughton say that the temporal limits of these contracts was increased to 50 years; however, our research revealed that the official national limit remains at 30 years as of 2016. We suspect that the actual maximum temporal length of contracts varies from province to province.

According to Meisner these land contracts established capitalist private property. He explains that (by the close of the 1980s) Chinese farmers believed that they would be able to freely hand down "their" land to their heirs, for several generations. Furthermore, contracted lands were sold, bought, rented, and mortgaged "as if they were fully alienable private property ... which established a de facto capitalist free market in land" (Meisner 1996: 230–231). Naughton disagrees.

Naughton argues that Mao gave property rights to the rural communes. In contrast, urban land was, and continues to be, owned by the Chinese communist government. Thus Deng could legally sell urban land and factories, but he could not sell rural land and factories. In support of his view that China does not have rural private property, Naughton explains that farm land (1) is subject to redistribution, (2) cannot be sold, and (3) cannot be used as collateral for bank loans. In the 1980s, communes often redistributed rural land to create farming plots for new rural dwellers. As communal governments were eliminated, local governments took over the right to redistribute land that was under contract. One empirical study found that 66% of the Chinese villages surveyed had undergone redistribution at least once and 25% had undergone redistribution three or more times. However, the primary reason for these redistributions shifted from making room for new village farmers to making room for development projects. Paying farmers the value of several years of crops in exchange for their land and then selling that land to developers for much, much more provided local governments with needed revenue and often personally enriched specific local government officials through bribes. On average, in 2011, local governments gained 26% of their government revenue from selling confiscated farm land to developers. China's national government is now very concerned because the amount of arable land has been shrinking and farmers protesting (Naughton 2007: 118–122, 214–215, 246–248 and Jonathan E. Leightner (*Ethics, Efficiency, and Macroeconomics in China from Mao to Xi* (Oxon, Routledge Press, 2017).

74 However, rural areas lost the medical and educational services that the communes had provided (Meisner, Maurice, *The Deng Xiaoping Era: An Inquiry into the Fate of Chinese Socialism 1978–1994* (New York: Hill and Wang, 1996), p. 247–248 and Naughton, Barry, The Chinese Economy: Transitions and Growth (Cambridge, Massachusetts, MIT Press, 2007), p. 243–246). Furthermore, dam and Irrigation systems were not maintained, contributing to flooding in northern and central China in 1998 (*Meisner, Maurice, Mao's China and After: A History of the People's Republic*, 3rd edition (New York; the Free Press, 1999), p. 466). As rural incomes rose, so did rural inequality (Meisner, 1999: 467).

75 Wong, "Interpreting Rural Industrial Growth in the Post-Mao Period," 3–30.

76 Kung, "The Decline of Township-and-Village Enterprises in China's Economic Transition," 569–84.

77 Oi, "Fiscal Reform and the Economic Foundations of Local State Corporatism," 99–126.

78 Between 1978 and 1984, rural agricultural plus industrial production increased 9% annually and labor productivity increased 5% annually, causing per capita rural income to double (Meisner, Maurice, *The Deng Xiaoping Era: An Inquiry into the Fate of Chinese Socialism 1978–1994* (New York: Hill and Wang, 1996), p. 235–236). During the Mao years, China's agricultural production grew 2.3 percent annually (Meisner, Maurice, *Mao's China and After: A History of the People's Republic*, 3rd edition (New York; the Free Press, 1999), p. 416). In the two years after Mao's death (1977 and 1978) China's grain production grew 2.2% annually. For the two years after implementing the household responsibility system (1983–1984), growth in grain production almost doubled to 4.1% annually (Naughton, Barry, *The Chinese Economy: Transitions and Growth* (Cambridge, Massachusetts, MIT Press, 2007), p. 242). The household responsibility system should receive some of the credit for the increase in agricultural growth for 1983–1984 (and some of the blame for the decline in that growth in 1985); however, other factors were also involved with that growth, chief of which was Green Revolution technology.

 The Green Revolution uses hybrid seeds that can produce double the output of traditional seeds, but to get that increase approximately double the amount of fertilizer and water must be used. Mao built the largest hybrid seed distribution and production system on the earth. Furthermore, during the Mao years, China's communes dug hundreds of kilometers of irrigation ditches. The only thing that China had insufficient supplies of for Green Revolution technology was fertilizer. Thus, when China increased importing under Deng, the importation of fertilizer producing plants was near the top of China's priority list. International trade made it possible for China to get the fertilizer needed to use Green Revolution technology (Naughton 2007: 252–263).

 In 1984, China enjoyed a record grain harvest of 407 million metric tons, but the 1985 harvest fell 6.9 percent to only 379 million tons – the largest annual decline since the famine of 1960. The harvest increased to 405 million tons in 1987 but fell to 394 million tons in 1988. Meisner (1996: 239) believes that the "marketization of the rural economy" caused the mid-1980s fall in grain production. Clearly the household responsibility system did not create sustained increased agricultural growth.

79   The figure measures China's rural population in 2015. The source is the World Bank. http://data.worldbank.org/indicator/SP.RUR.TOTL

80   Hua Guofeng started the first special economic zones (SEZs), but Deng strongly promoted them. The purpose of the special economic zones (SEZs) was for China to acquire foreign technology and capital without having to spend her scarce foreign reserves. Critics saw these SEZs as similar to the treaty ports taken from China after the Opium War, as a waste of money, and as hotbeds for corruption. Deng Xiaoping personally investigated Shenzhen, the biggest SEZ, and declared it a great success. Deng claimed that, between 1980 and 1984, Shenzhen signed in excess of 3,000 contracts worth US$ 2.3 billion with investors based in fifty countries. Furthermore, during that time, the number of manufacturing firms in Shenzhen SEZ increased from 26 to 500 and total Shenzhen SEZ output increased 29-fold while the Chinese workers employed there were paid five times the average Chinese urban wage (Meisner, Maurice, *The Deng Xiaoping Era: An Inquiry into the Fate of Chinese Socialism 1978–1994* (New York: Hill and Wang, 1996), p. 277).

   Historically, China's paramount leaders have lost power when their signature policies have failed (Leightner, Jonathan, *Ethics, Efficiency, and Macroeconomics in China from Mao to Xi* (Oxon, Routledge Press, 2017). Therefore, China's leaders try to make sure that their policies at least look successful. For the case of Shenzhen's SEZ, most of Deng's claims (given in the previous paragraph) are exaggerations or lies. Most of the "3,000 contracts" were mere letters of intent which never produced results. Two thirds of Shenzhen's capital came from inside China, not from foreign firms. The Chinese government's investment in building Shenzhen's infrastructure significantly exceeded total non-government investment in that SEZ. Furthermore, the reported value of Shenzhen's total output included what the Chinese government spent to build Shenzhen's infrastructure. Moreover, only ten percent of the production entities in Shenzhen used advanced technology, Shenzhen used more foreign exchange than it earned, and Shenzhen was a center for the illegal smuggling of foreign goods into China (Meisner 1996: 278–279).

   The SEZ on Hainan Island was an unusually embarrassing case of SEZ corruption and smuggling. Officials there borrowed more than 500 million US dollars in foreign currencies, purchased 89,000 cars and trucks, 122,000 motorcycles, three million televisions, and 250,000 VCRs, which were smuggled into China and illegally sold for three or four times their purchase prices (Meisner 1996: 281). When the corruption of Hainan Island's SEZ was revealed, the officials in charge of that SEZ merely got their hands slapped, encouraging the spread of corruption throughout all of China (Meisner 1996: 324–325 see also Vogel, Ezra F., *Deng Xiaoping: and the Transformation of China* (Cambridge, Massachusetts: Harvard University Press, 2011), pp. 412–418). The children of China's highest leaders, especially the sons of Zhao Ziyang and Deng Xiaoping, were extremely successful at making money from corruption (see Meisner 1996: 326–336 for details).

81   In 1984, Deng was determined to allow markets more freedom in urban areas. Therefore, the communist party reduced its interference with firm decisions, encouraged firms to adopt western managerial methods, told firms to maximize profits as their sole goal, and cut the amount of direct government funding provided to firms, forcing firms to turn to bank loans. Since China's banks are state owned, this last point was of debatable value especially in light of the fact that the government told its banks to prevent bankruptcies and greater unemployment by lending money to troubled firms. (Meisner, Maurice,

The Deng Xiaoping Era: An Inquiry into the Fate of Chinese Socialism 1978–1994 (New York: Hill and Wang, 1996), pp. 288–289, 293 and Meisner, Maurice, Mao's China and After: A History of the People's Republic, 3rd edition (New York; the Free Press, 1999), pp. 469–470).

Firms would earn more profits if they could fire unproductive workers. Thus Deng wanted to "smash the iron rice bowl" meaning he wanted to eliminate job security so that a totally free labor market could emerge (Meisner 1999: 470). However, a majority of the Politburo insisted that only new hires not be promised job security while those already employed at state owned enterprise would retain their benefits and tenure (Meisner 1996: 290–292 and Meisner 1999: 472).

82 Dong, "China's Price Reform," 291–300.

83 In 1984, Deng finally succeeded in getting the Politburo to approve partial price reform. The agreed upon plan consisted of (1) the prices of coal, oil, steel, and other essential inputs continuing to be fixed by the government, (2) the prices of industrial outputs fluctuating between upper and lower bounds which were fixed by the government, (3) and the prices of agricultural products and most consumer goods fluctuating freely (Meisner, Maurice, *The Deng Xiaoping Era: An Inquiry into the Fate of Chinese Socialism 1978–1994* (New York: Hill and Wang, 1996), p. 292). However, after price controls on tobacco and alcohol were eliminated in July 1988, their prices surged two hundred percent (Vogel, Ezra F., *Deng Xiaoping: and the Transformation of China* (Cambridge, Massachusetts: Harvard University Press, 2011), p. 470). In August 1988, a massive number of Chinese withdrew their bank deposits and stocked up on supplies after the *People's Daily* announced the government's plan to soon eliminate more price controls. Store shelves were emptied and street demonstrations occurred (Vogel 2011: 470). Deng's plan to free more prices was not implemented, and Deng and Zhao Ziyang lost some political power (Vogel 2011: 471).

According to Meisner (Maurice, *Mao's China and After: A History of the People's Republic*, 3rd edition (New York; the Free Press, 1999), p. 470) inflation was less than 0.5 percent annually under Mao). Unused to inflation, the Chinese were very upset when inflation hit 9% in 1985 and 7% in 1986. Furthermore these nation-wide inflation rates understate the problem for major urban areas – Beijing's consumer prices increased an average of 30% in 1985 (Meisner 1996: 293). When Deng's pro-market reforms resulted in excess inflation, Chen Yun persuaded the Politburo to return to price controls and austerity policies (Meisner 1996: 294–296). Chen's austerity program reduced inflation and increased urban unemployment (Meisner 1999: 471).

84 Under Chen Yun's inflation-fighting austerity program many government institutions (from schools to the People's Liberation Army) experienced cuts in funding. In response, Deng suggested that they replace state support with business profits. The Ministry of Public Security earned profits through hotels. Among other ventures, the State Security Ministry ran an import-export business and an employment agency. Several police agencies earned money through manufacturing. Some university academic departments ran restaurants, and police agencies started manufacturing. Grade school teachers were allowed to sell candy and notebooks to their students. The People's Liberation Army (PLA) ran more than 20,000 for profit firms including the exportation of weapons, the transportation of non-military goods, the hotel business, and manufacturing (Meisner, Maurice, *The Deng Xiaoping Era: An Inquiry into the Fate of Chinese Socialism 1978–1994* (New York: Hill and Wang, 1996), p. 333–336 see also Vogel, Ezra F., *Deng Xiaoping: and the Transformation of China* (Cambridge, Massachusetts: Harvard University Press, 2011), pp. 548–551). Forcing some government agencies to earn their own funds resulted in some awkward inconsistencies. For example,

the All-China Federation of Women earned profits by importing and using Russian prostitutes, contrary to its founding purpose which was to combat sexual inequality (Meisner 1996: 335–336).

85 Vladimir Lenin experimented with leasing based socialist markets from 1921–29 in the Soviet Union. Managers were granted considerable discretion, but the state tried to guide and direct their behavior with micro-incentives and directive controls. The paradigm was called the New Economic Policy (NEP). See Rosefielde, *Russian Economy from Lenin to Putin.*

86 The Deng government tried several different ways to incentivize managers towards the maximization of profits. From 1979 to 1983, firms were allowed to keep a percent (which was usually less than 10 percent) of the profits. From 1983 to 1986, firms could retain between ten to fifty percent of any improvement in profits over what was earned the previous year. From 1986 to 1989, firms would negotiate with government officials for a target level of profits and the firm could retain between 50% and 100% of any profits they earned above that target. This last approach increased government's involvement and opened wide the door to corruption – firm managers could bribe the government official with whom they were negotiating for a low contracted level of profits, increasing the manager's ultimate take home pay (Naughton, Barry, *The Chinese Economy: Transitions and Growth* (Cambridge, Massachusetts, MIT Press, 2007), pp. 311–313).

87 The term *market communism* for most Marxists is an oxymoron. Markets from their perspective are transactionary mechanisms used by capitalists to pursue private gain at the community's (workers') expense, whereas it is claimed that communism liberates the masses from market subjugation, inequality and injustice. Communism fosters the actualization of human potential through reciprocally empowering communal support. Markets and communism from the purist viewpoint are mutually exclusive.

88 Two children per family became the legal norm January 1, 2016.

89 On April 15, 1989, Hu Yaobang, who was relatively tolerant of protesters and an advocate for greater democracy, died from heart failure. On April 17th, five hundred Beijing University students honored Hu by beginning a march through Beijing to Tiananmen Square (the symbolic center of China's government). As they marched they sang the Communist "Internationale" and other revolutionary songs and many more students joined them. Four thousand students and youths arrived in Tiananmen Square early on April 18th. One thousand students demanded that the National People's Congress accept their petition and began a sit-in protest (Meisner, Maurice, *The Deng Xiaoping Era: An Inquiry into the Fate of Chinese Socialism 1978–1994* (New York: Hill and Wang, 1996), pp. 404–405).

Responding to the swelling number of protesters, the government prohibited the public from being in Tiananmen Square on April 22, the day of Hu Yaobang's funeral. To enforce that prohibition, the police and army arrived at the square at 6am on April 22, where they found 10,000 students already obstructing the Gate of Heavenly Peace and approximately 30,000 non-students and 70,000 students in Tiananmen Square. After the funeral, more than one million citizens lined the route to the cemetery and 100,000 people in Tiananmen Square stood silently (Meisner 1996: 406–407).

90 On April 23rd, the students in Tiananmen Square proclaimed the establishment of a "Provisional Autonomous Federation of Beijing University Students." On April 24th, students at twenty-one Beijing universities and colleges began a student strike. Student demands included four things: (1) a free press, (2) democracy, (3) non-interference in the formation and operations of "autonomous" organizations as long as they did oppose or hurt the communist party, and (4) the public revelation and explanation of the assets

of China's leaders and of their families, (Meisner, Maurice, *The Deng Xiaoping Era: An Inquiry into the Fate of Chinese Socialism 1978–1994* (New York: Hill and Wang, 1996), pp. 406, 408, 412–414, 422, and 445–447). This fourth demand was a direct consequence of the massive amounts of corruption involving the families of China's leaders, especially Deng Xiaoping's and Zhao Ziyang's. The students were careful to repeatedly express their support for the Communist Party of China; however, they desired a Communist party that was less corrupt.

As requested by Deng, the *People's Daily* published, on April 26th, an editorial denouncing the protests and accusing them of being the result of a conspiracy aimed at sabotaging the Communist Party by taking advantage of grief in order to sow dissension, create chaos, and destroy political unity and stability. The editorial advised an immediate cessation of all illegal demonstrations, meetings, and organizations. The day after the editorial was published, April 27th, the people of Beijing publically showed their support of the 80,000 students who marched through the streets of Beijing protesting the editorial. By the end of that day, the government announced that it would meet with student leaders. The students insisted that the meeting be broadcast on TV. The government agreed, and the televised meeting was held on April 29th. For the first time, the citizens of China saw Chinese leaders publically accused of bureaucratic privilege, corruption, and the suppression of the truth. However, the government stood by its absolute refusal to allow "autonomous" organizations. What had started as a student movement in Beijing soon became a nation-wide movement involving not only students, but also workers and other citizens (Meisner 1996: 410–421).

Soviet President Mikhail Gorbachev, who at that time was extremely popular in the USSR and around the world, had agreed to visit China on May 15, 1989. Deng Xiaoping, who was suffering from declining popularity within China, wanted the world's press to take his picture with Gorbachev's during a welcoming ceremony in Tiananmen Square. While waiting for Gorbachev's visit, the international press observed and reported on the student protests (Meisner, Maurice, *Mao's China and After: A History of the People's Republic*, 3rd edition (New York; the Free Press, 1999), pp. 504–505).

In the center of Tiananmen Square on May 13th, five hundred students started a hunger strike. Defying repeated orders that they vacate the Square, the students caused the elaborate Gorbachev welcoming ceremony planned for the square to be replaced by a brief ceremony at the airport. China's leadership was embarrassed as the world's press showed that the communist government was not even in control of the center of China's power structure (Meisner 1996: 425–430).

After industrial workers organized an "autonomous" organization for themselves, the "Capital Workers' Autonomous Federation," Deng argued that martial law must be declared. When Zhao Ziyang was the only leader who objected to martial law, he fled to Tiananmen Square, arriving at 4am on May 19th where he was observed crying (Meisner 1996: 431–432). Zhao told the students, "We were once young too, and we all had such bursts of energy. We also staged demonstrations … [and] we also did not think of the consequences" (Feigon, Lee, *China Rising* (Chicago: Ivan R. Dee, 1990), pp. 209–210 as cited in Meisner 1996: 432). Zhao begged the students to abandon the Square.

In response to the government's declaration of martial law, the citizens of Beijing barricaded all the streets that emptied into Tiananmen Square. On May 21, 1989, a million protestors against martial law were in Tiananmen Square (Meisner 1996: 436–454). Also on May 21st, seven retired but high ranking military leaders submitted an open letter to Deng Xiaoping that explained "the People's Liberation Army belongs to the people" and "it cannot stand in opposition to the people, much less oppress the people, and it absolutely cannot open fire on the people and create a blood-shedding incident. In order to prevent further worsening of the situation, troops should not enter the city" (as quoted in Meisner 1996: 437). Members of Beijing's secret police and elite security organizations publically joined the antigovernment protests. Sympathy protests spread throughout China. In Canton, 500,000 people marched to show support for the students on May 24th (Meisner 1996: 438).

In the first days of June 1989, two hundred thousand People's Liberation Army troops converged on Beijing. Many of the protesters left the Square out of fear, but approximately 5000 people still remained. On June 3rd, at dusk, forty thousand troops with armored personnel carriers and tanks invaded Beijing. At 10:30 pm, unarmed citizens who were blocking the path of the troops were fired upon. Troops began reaching Tiananmen Square at approximately midnight. All protestors were cleared out of the square by 5am on June 4th (Meisner 1996: 440–463).

91 The possibility of *market socialism* was debated in the nineteenth century, but rejected by most communists in 1929 when Stalin forcibly collectivized the Soviet Union. The idea was resurrected in the west by Oscar Lange in 1936–37, and has been influential since. See Lange and Taylor, *On the Economic Theory of Socialism*, 1938. Stalin was impressed by Lange's theory. He summoned him to Moscow for consultations and Lange lobbied Franklin Roosevelt on Stalin's behalf regarding the government of postwar Poland. From 1961–65 Lange served as one of four acting Chairmen of the Polish State Council (Head of State).

92 Under Jiang Zemin, China stopped all efforts aimed at material balance planning and eliminated all remaining price controls (Naughton, Barry, *The Chinese Economy: Transitions and Growth* (Cambridge, Massachusetts, MIT Press, 2007), p. 101). Also under Jiang, China established a stock market, privatized many State Owned Enterprises (SOEs), allowed other SOEs to go bankrupt, established boards of directors for corporations, and allowed the unconstrained buying and selling of companies, buildings, and equipment (Naughton 2007).

Under Jiang Zemin, the primary ways that China deviated from a totally free market/capitalist system benefitted capitalist, at the expense of labor and consumers (recall that Marx believed that the government, under capitalism, would be a tool of the capitalist class). These pro-capitalist deviations from a totally free market included (1) forbidding labor strikes, (2) outlawing labor unions that are not sponsored by the government, (3) forbidding China's masses from investing overseas while fixing a below equilibrium interest rate for domestic savings, (4) fixing an exchange rate below equilibrium, and (5) maintaining government ownership and control of a few important industries that were natural monopolies, provided key public goods, or were vital to national security.

93 The 1993 Company Law established the legal foundation required for the gradual transformation of state owned enterprises (SOEs) into limited-liability corporations, controlled by boards of directors (Naughton, Barry, *The Chinese Economy: Transitions and Growth* (Cambridge, Massachusetts, MIT Press, 2007), pp. 104, 301, and 314–318). The 15th Communist Party Congress in 1997 gave local government officials permission to pursue mergers and acquisitions, bankruptcies, and auctions and sales of state owned enterprises in their jurisdiction (Naughton 2007: 105). A Securities Law was passed in 1999 which set up a nation-wide system of security supervisors (Naughton 2007: 104).

Town and Village Enterprises (TVEs) were also transformed in the 1990s. TVEs initially were owned by communes and were one of the most dynamic parts of China's economy. Realizing the tremendous potential profits of their TVEs, managers of these TVEs became greedy and wanted to keep all the profits for themselves. Knowing that the co-owners would be more likely to sell if the TVEs looked less successful, some managers would pay all the firm's bills while suggesting that those who owe money to the firm delay payment. More importantly, the manager's family could operate firms that either bought the output of the TVE or sold parts and supplies to the TVE at prices that siphoned the TVE profits into the manager's family. This type of arrangement is called "tunneling" and some of the managers of both SOEs and TVEs practiced it. After making the TVE appear less profitable, the manager could often convinced the TVE's co-owners to sell. The manager, or a family member or friend, would purchase the firm at a discounted price, transforming it into a private enterprise (Naughton 2007: 106, 286–292, and 322–323).

By the end of 2004, private firms in cities (not including foreign invested firms) employed 55,000,000 workers while SOEs employed less than 30,000,000 (Naughton 2007: 106). A 2004 census counted 947,000 private firms and 5,300,000 unincorporated family businesses in China that were involved with industrial production, which together employed 59,000,000 workers (Naughton 2007: 304).

94 Zhu served as the fifth Premier of the People's Republic of China from March 1998 to March 2003.

95 Jiang Zemin held the position of General Secretary of the Chinese Communist Party from 1989 to 2002.

96 Hu Jintao succeeded Jiang Zemin 2002 to 2012. Hu's successor was Xi Jinping, former Vice Chairman of the Communist Party.

97 http://princeling.askdefine.com. China had 80 billionaires in 2009, a quarter of whom derived their wealth from real estate (http://www.forbes.com/2009/11/05/china-new-billionaire.html). See Forsythe, "China's Billionaire Lawmakers Make U.S. Peers Look Like Paupers": "The richest 70 members of China's legislature added more to their wealth last year than the combined net worth of all 535 members of the U.S. Congress, the president and his Cabinet, and the nine Supreme Court justices. The net worth of the 70 richest delegates in China's National People's Congress, which opens its annual session on March 5, rose to 565.8 billion yuan ($89.8 billion) in 2011, a gain of $11.5 billion from 2010, according to figures from the Hurun Report, which tracks the country's wealthy. That compares to the $7.5 billion net worth of all 660 top officials in the three branches of the U.S. government. The income gain by NPC members reflects the imbalances in economic growth in China, where per capita annual income in 2010 was $2,425, less than in Belarus and a fraction of the $37,527 in the U.S. The disparity points to the challenges that China's new generation of leaders, to be named this year, faces in countering a rise in social unrest fueled by illegal land grabs and corruption. The National People's Congress, whose annual meeting will run for a week and a half, is legally the highest governmental body in China. While the legislature, with about 3,000 members, is often derided as a rubberstamp parliament, its members are some of China's most powerful politicians and executives, wielding power in their home provinces and weighing in on proposals such as whether to impose a nationwide property tax. Hurun, a Shanghai-based publisher of magazines targeted at the Chinese luxury consumer, uses publicly available information such as corporate filings to compile its annual list of the richest people in China. Hurun crosschecked the data with the government's list of NPC members. Zong Qinghou, chairman of beverage-maker Hangzhou Wahaha Group and China's second-richest person, with a family fortune of 68 billion yuan, is a member. So is Wu Yajun, chairwoman of Beijing-based Longfor Properties Co. She has family wealth of 42 billion yuan, according to the Hurun Report. China's top political leaders, including President Hu Jintao and Wen, don't disclose their personal finances or those of their families."

98 China's Gini coefficient was 0.28 in 1983. At that time, China was one of the most equal countries on the earth (Sweden's and Japan's Ginis were 0.25 while Germany's was 0.28). It is much easier for smaller countries (like Japan, Sweden, and Germany) to be equal than it is for very large countries like China.

China's Gini coefficient in 2001 had surged to 0.447 making China less equal than Indonesia (Gini = 0.34), India (Gini = 0.325), South Korea (Gini = 0.32) and the USA (Gini = 0.408 in 2000) (Naughton, Barry, *The Chinese Economy: Transitions and Growth* (Cambridge, Massachusetts, MIT Press, 2007), pp. 217–218). Naughton explains, "China's increase in inequality is unprecedented. ... there may be no other case where a society's income distribution has deteriorated so much, so fast."

After 2001, China's Gini continued to rise. According to Gabriel Wildau and Tom Mitchell (January 14, 2016, "China Income Inequality among World's Worst," *Financial Times*), 33% of China's wealth is held by the richest 1% of China's households and the poorest 25% of China's households own only 1% of China's wealth. In 2012, China's Gini coefficient for income was 0.49.

Among the world's 25 largest countries by population for which the World Bank tracks Gini data, only South Africa and Brazil are higher at 0.63 and 0.53 respectively. The figure for the US is 0.41, while Germany is 0.3 (Wildau and Mitchell 2016).

However according to China's Statistics Bureau China's Gini was only 0.469 in 2014. In contrast, economists working at Southwest University of Finance and Economics in Chengdu estimated China's 2010 income Gini to be 0.61 (Wildau and Mitchell 2016).

Gini coefficients underestimate the decrease in equality that occurred after Mao's death because they do not show the widening gap between government-provided services in rural and urban areas. For example, in 1998, the Ministry of Health reported that rural residents pay "for 87 percent of their health care expenses themselves" while urban residents pay "for only 44 percent of their own health care expenses" (Naughton 2007: 246). Meanwhile, during the 1990s, the cost of a hospital stay in China increased six fold and the cost of being seen at a health clinic increased eight fold (Naughton 2007: 246). Thus the actual increase in China's inequality was much more severe than the above reported increases in China's Gini coefficient show.

99 The leaseholds are implicit because the CEOs aren't required to pay fixed rents. Instead they must pay the freehold owner (Communist Party) whatever is demanded.

100 This principle includes the sale of dividend streams to private portfolio investors.

101 Xu, "State-Owned Enterprises in China: How Big Are They?" World Bank Blog, January 19, 2011. There were 154,000 SOEs in 2008.

102 Tselichtchev and Debroux, *Asia's Turning Point: An Introduction to Asia's Dynamic Economies at the Dawn of the New Century*.

103 Mukherjee, Gopalan, and Molla, "Uncovering China's SOEs".

104 For a recent assessment see Mukherjee, Gopalan and Molla, "Uncovering China's SOEs." Bloomberg, April 28, 2016.

105 See "Of Emperors and Kings: China's State-Owned Enterprises Are on the March," *The Economist*, November 11, 2011: "... how, in sectors ranging from telecommunications to textiles, the government has quietly obstructed market forces. It steers cheap credit to local champions. It enforces rules selectively, to keep private-sector rivals in their place. State firms such as China Telecom can dominate local markets without running afoul of antitrust authorities; but when foreigners such as Coca-Cola try to acquire local firms, they can be blocked. ..." Also see Hsueh, *China's Regulatory State: A New Strategy for Globalization*.

106 Collective firms, discussed in the literature on "hybrid" property rights, usually have considerable autonomy. Huchet and Richet see most of these firms (TVEs) transitioning to wholly private enterprises (Huchet and Richet, "Between Bureaucracy and Market").

107 In 2005, for the first time since 1949, private banks were officially sanctioned in twenty locations within China. In December 2006, China's government permitted foreign owned banks to provide domestic currency services to Chinese citizens throughout all of China (Naughton, Barry, *The Chinese Economy: Transitions and Growth* (Cambridge, Massachusetts, MIT Press, 2007), pp. 459, 449). However, state owned banks dominate China banking industry even in 2017. Wen Jiabao, China's premier under Hu Jintao, strongly condemned China's banks, called them monopolies, and insisted that increased competition occur in China's banking (Leightner, Jonathan, *Ethics, Efficiency, and Macroeconomics in China from Mao to Xi* (Oxon: Routledge Press, 2017).

108 The term rent-seeking means that privileged individuals try to acquire non-competitive state contracts which provide them with unearned income. Rent-granting is the granting of these non-competitive state contracts, with some kind of payoff to the grantor.

109 Cf. Bukharin, *Building Up Socialism*.

110 Buckley, "Briton Killed after Threat to Expose Chinese Leader's Wife." Yahoo/News, April 17, 2012. Gu Kailai, wife of Bo Xilai, one-time Politburo aspirant and CPC Chongqing Committee Secretary, was arrested and charged with killing British businessman Neil Heywood because he refused to move a large sum of money abroad, and threatened to expose her. This story may have come to light because the Politburo is currently engaged in a campaign to discredit Bo's efforts to revive Maoism (Red Culture Movement) in Chongqing. Bo's reforms are sometimes labeled the "Chongqing model."

111 It can be argued, however, that the system victimizes peasants and those who flee from rural areas to cities in several different ways. For example, rural governments often redistribute farm land in order to create large plots of land to sell to developers. These land sales have become the largest source of government revenue in some areas, contributing up to 37 percent of total rural government revenue (Deininger, Klaus and Songqing Jin (2009), "Securing Property Rights in Transition: Lessons from Implementation of China's Rural Land Contracting Law" *Journal of Economic Behavior and Organization* 70(1–2): 22–38). According to one big survey study, at least one redistribution of land occurred in 66 percent of villages and three or more redistributions had occurred in 25 percent of villages (Naughton, Barry, *The Chinese Economy: Transitions and Growth* (Cambridge, Massachusetts, MIT Press, 2007), p. 120). If a particular plot of land is currently not worked, then that land is more likely be taken in a redistribution. However, if a rural migrant can find a city job, he or she can earn many times more than the farm would produce. Knowing this, many farmers migrate to cities but command their young children to stay behind to keep the farm land producing. This has produced many abandoned and traumatized rural children (Leightner, Jonathan, Ethics, *Efficiency, and Macroeconomics in China from Mao to Xi* (Oxon: Routledge Press, 2017).

The gap between what a farmer can earn working in a city versus on the farm is so large that China has developed an enormous illegal "floating" population (liudong renkou). A migrant is part of China's floating population if he or she lives at least six months outside of where his or her household is registered. According to the 2000 census. China's floating population included 144,000,000 Chinese, almost 12% of China's population. 79,000,000 of these migrants were both long term and long distance. China's long distance floating population increased "from 7 million in 1982, to 22 million in 1990, to 79 million in 2000" (Naughton 2007: 130).

Because living outside of one's official place of residence is illegal, migrants are not helped by the police nor can migrants use the hospitals, schools, and other social services given to registered urbanites. Because illegal migrants have no legal protection, many profit maximizing employers hire migrants on Monday, promising to pay them for a week's work on Friday. When Friday comes, no pay is given. If the migrant goes to the police, the police merely deport the migrant to his registered home (at best). Hiring workers who are not paid increases profits, ceteris paribus. When 8,000 migrants were interviewed in one 2003 study covering eight different provinces, 48 percent of the migrants reported that they had been promised wages that were never paid. According to the National Trade Union there are approximately US$ 12 billion in unpaid wages in China (Naughton 2007: 125).

112 The system disciplines labor and prohibits strikes to the benefit of corporations. It also has ignored labor protection and safety for the same reason. For example, in 1995, coal mines produced in more than half of China's counties. In 1995, 46% of China's total coal output was the combined production of 34,700 individually run mines and 34,200 village-collective-run mines. The owners of the mines did not adequately invest in safety equipment or in the shoring up of mine tunnels for doing so would have reduced profits which were small to begin with due to the competitive nature of the industry. Thus it is not surprising that, in 2004, a total of 6,027 accidental deaths occurred in China's coal mines (Naughton, Barry, *The Chinese Economy: Transitions and Growth* (Cambridge, Massachusetts, MIT Press, 2007), p. 338–339).

113 Rosefielde, "The Illusion of Westernization in Russia and China," 495–513.

114 Solow, "Technical Change and the Aggregate Production Function," 312–20.

115 This deduction could be mistaken if China develops a miraculously potent domestic R&D mechanism.

116 The accolade was given by the Party in October 2016. Buckley, "Xi Jinping Is China's 'Core' Leader: Here's What It Means." New York Times, October 30, 2016.

117 Xi began promoting the slogan in November 2012 immediately after taking the office of general secretary. Since then, use of the phrase has become widespread in official announcements and has come to embody the political ideology of Xi's regime.

118 Kuhn interprets Xi's Chinese Dream to mean a diversion of political ideology from egalitarianism to a relatively more libertarian individualist approach. "Modernization" means China regaining its position as a world leader in science and technology as well as in economics and business; the resurgence of Chinese civilization, culture and military might; and China participating actively in all areas of human endeavor. Some government officials and activists view the Chinese Dream as a need for economic and political reform. Sustaining China's economic growth requires economic reform encompassing urbanization, the reduction of government bureaucracy, and weakening the power of special interests. Chinese liberals have defined the Chinese Dream as a dream of constitutionalism. Both Xi Jinping and Premier Li Keqiang support economic reform, but have shied away from discussing political reform.

119 Central Party School/Central Committee of the Communist Party of China, "The Chinese Dream infuses Socialism with Chinese Characteristics with New Energy", Qiushi. https://chinacopyrightandmedia.wordpress.com/2013/05/06/the-chinese-dream-infuses-socialism-with-chinese-characteristics-with-new-energy/.

120 Kuhn, Robert, "Xi Jinping's Chinese Dream." New York times, June 4, 2013.

121 Jonathan Leightner (*Ethics, Efficiency, and Macroeconomics in China from Mao to Xi* (Oxon, Routledge Press, 2017) chapter 11) explains Xi's increased control of the internet, television, and film. In essence, Xi prohibits anything that he does not like even if it is the truth. For example, he prohibited accurate reporting of the stock market crashes of 2015 and 2016. Xi's government has repeatedly threatened to go after anyone who spread rumors that could hurt China, her unity, her communist party, and/or her interests. For example, when Caijing news magazine reported that 76.8 percent (a total of US$ 9.9 billion) of donations for Sichuan's 2008 earthquake relief was taken by the government, the article was deleted and the rest of China's media received the following instructions: "No website may carry the Caijing story 'Of 65.2 Billion Yuan in Wenchuan Earthquake Donations, 80% Went to Government Coffers; Where 50.1 Billion Went is Unclear.' If you have already republished the article, please remove it immediately" (http://chinadigitaltimes.net/2016/05/mintrue-not-carry-story-missing-earthquake-donations).

Furthermore, Xi's government has forbidden schools for younger students that are for profit and has legally insisted that all schools be run "in a way supportive of socialism." In July 2015, Xi's government conducted a nation-wide sweep rounding up human-right lawyers. In April 2016, China's legislature passed a law severely restricting foreign nonprofits, stating "any activities of foreign nonprofits that threaten national security or ethnic harmony will be punished." Some Chinese officials see foreign ideologies and western ideas as threats to national security and to ethnic harmony.

In November 2015, the Chinese government conducted a conference in the capital which discussed Christianity in China. Christianity is the biggest non-government group in China. Some experts believe there are in excess of 100,000,000 Christians in China already and that this number is increasing by 7% each year. The Pew Research center believes there are only 67,000,000 Christians in China (and 87,000,000 members of the Chinese Communist Party.

In July 2016, the communist leaders of Guizhou province announced that all "welfare or any old-age insurance" would be denied those who "gathered again" as Christians. Chinese law forbids the giving of any religious education to anyone younger than 18 (they cannot even attend state-approved churches). Guizhou authorities have threatened law suits against anyone bringing a minor to church and a barring from attending college or a military academy for any minor who attends a church service. In 2016, the Organization Department of the Chinese Communist party publicized a new regulation forbidding all Communist Party Members (even retired ones) from being religious:

There are clear rules that retired cadres and party members cannot believe in religion, cannot take part in religious activities, and must absolutely fight against cults. ... [Retired officials should] maintain a high degree of consistency, in thought, in political views and in action, with the central party committee which is headed by Xi Jinping (http://www.bbc.com/news/world-asia-china-35502211).

Notice how China's government is now being defined as "headed by Xi Jinping" instead of headed by the Standing Committee of the Politburo.

122 In 2015, China's stock regulator gave permission to brokers to securitize margin loans (package and sell them to investors). This securitization is similar to the creation of financial derivatives that caused the sub-prime crisis in the USA in 2007-2008 (Jonathan Leightner (*Ethics, Efficiency, and Macroeconomics in China from Mao to Xi* (Oxon, Routledge Press, 2017)).

123 Jonathan Leightner (*Ethics, Efficiency, and Macroeconomics in China from Mao to Xi* (Oxon, Routledge Press, 2017) chapter 12) explains several aspects of China's economy that

are related to China's standard of living including wages, the price of housing, and the return from investments. Private sector wages in China increased 12.3 percent in 2011 followed by 14 percent in 2012. Between 2008 and 2012, China's manufacturing wages rose 71 percent. The pay of migrant workers also increased by double digit percentages between 2010 and 2014. These pay increases are a direct result of an increasingly severe Chinese labor shortage. At the end of 2014, for every 100 job seekers, there were 115 job openings.

In 2014, Xi Jinping's government limited top executive pay in the 100 SOEs that China's central government directly controls to no more than ten times the average salary of the company's employees. This should raise the average standard of living in China. Furthermore, Xi's government is encouraging local governments to follow the same rule at the thousands of companies controlled by them. In a conflicting move, Xi's government started to suppress wage increases in 2016 by changing the rules for setting minimum wages in such a way that minimum wages would be drastically reduced (see chapter 12 of Leightner, 2017, for details). Chinese minimum wages range from US$ 1.15/hour in small cities to US$ 2.87/hour in Beijing in comparison to a US federal minimum wage of US$ 7.25/hour. Guangdong imposed a freeze for two years on minimum wages in February of 2016.

In many countries, migrating from rural areas to a city would improve one's standard of living due to greater access to public services and greater opportunities. However, most Chinese migrants are prohibited from using city-provided services and the price of urban housing is often prohibitively expensive for migrants. Leightner (2017, chapter 12) explains how China's limited investment opportunities for the Chinese masses has led to the purchase of empty apartments as investments, creating several huge ghost towns while driving up the price housing to prohibitive levels for the very poor. In 2013, Beijing's housing prices rose 16% per year and rents 12% per year. In November 2013, Beijing residential property sold for a median price of US$ 4,500/meter^2, and rents were US$ 9.50/meter^2. In that month, the average yearly income was slightly greater than US$ 6,000 in China. "That makes Beijing homes almost three times as expensive for Chinese as buying a home in New York City is for Americans." Because many migrants are paid too little to afford even a small apartment, many of them rent small sections of basements (usually less than 5 meters^2) that have neither heating nor air conditioning. In December 2014, Beijing ordered the sealing of manhole covers "after local media discovered a group of people living in the sewers below." One person (52 years old) said that the sewer had been his home for at least ten years http://www.reuters.com/article/us-china-property-basement-idUSBREA040GD20140105.

The standard of living of migrants is also undercut by a lack of health care insurance. China claims that 95 percent of Chinese citizens are covered by health insurance. However, to access this insurance, one must be in the area where they are registered to live. This means that migrants do not have insurance that they can actually use. A Chinese government survey reported that a mere 18 percent of migrants have access to employer health insurance because where they are registered to live is far from where they work.

124 State Council. The Silk Road Economic Belt and the twenty-first-century Maritime Silk Road, also known as The Belt and Road; One Belt, One Road (abbreviated OBOR), or the Belt and Road Initiative, is a development strategy and framework proposed by Chinese paramount leader Xi Jinping that focuses on connectivity and cooperation among countries primarily between the People's Republic of China and the rest of Eurasia, which consists of two main components, the land-based "Silk Road

Economic Belt" (SREB) and oceangoing "Maritime Silk Road" (MSR). The strategy underlines China's push to take a bigger role in global affairs.

125 Qin Shi Huang built a large section of China's Great Wall. The earliest segment dates to the seventh century BCE.

126 The Asian Infrastructure Investment Bank (AIIB) is an international financial institution that aims to support the building of infrastructure in the Asia-Pacific region. The bank has 57 member states (all "Founding Members") and was proposed as an initiative by the government of China.

127 Zhang, "Beijing's Master Plan for the South China Sea.", http://foreignpolicy .com/2015/06/23/south_china_sea_beijing_retreat_new_strategy/.

128 Office of the Secretary of Defense, Annual Report to Congress: Military and Security Developments Involving the People's Republic of China 2016, April 2016. http:// www.defense.gov/Portals/1/Documents/pubs/2016%20China%20Military%20 Power%20Report.pdf.

129 Jonathan Leightner (*Ethics, Efficiency, and Macroeconomics in China from Mao to Xi* (Oxon, Routledge Press, 2017) chapter 13) explains how China used her domination of the world's production of rare earth metals in her conflict with Japan over the islands that Japan calls the Senkaku Island and China calls the Diaoyudao Islands. Chapter 14 of Leightner (2017) explains China's conflicts with several nations over the South China Sea. His analysis of the South China Sea includes (1) China's claim to almost the entire sea and her building of artificial islands there (2) the January 2013 Permanent Court of Arbitration in The Hague's ruling against China's sea claims there and China's belligerent response to that ruling, (3) China's military confrontations with the USA and Vietnam in that sea, (4) China's establishment of military installations on the islands she has built there, (5) the hacking of the screens and sound systems at Vietnam's airports in Hanoi and Ho Chi Minh City to broadcast anti-Vietnamese and anti-Philippine messages about that sea, and (6) China's strong use of both carrots and sticks to get other South China Sea claimants to acquiesce to China's views. Leightner (2017, chapter 14) also explains the changes that Xi Jinping has introduced to China's military including (1) Xi's efforts to curb corruption in China's military and to force it to focus solely upon winning wars, (2) his setting up a joint command structure with himself in charge that can coordinate all of China's military divisions, (3) his shifting China's military from solely a defensive organization to one capable of offensive actions, (4) his building of more Chinese submarines and aircraft carriers, (5) his creation of a missile that can destroy the flight deck of a US aircraft carrier, and (6) his efforts to create cyber defensive and offensive military capabilities.

130 Gorky, *A Sky Blue Life*.

131 Xi Jinping launched a campaign to increase public participation in China's stock market, but continued banning public investment abroad. He sanctioned the creation of "wealth-management" products for rich bank clients, circumventing ceilings imposed on interest rates paid to saving bank depositors. Ninety million Chinese responded to Xi Jinping's call to invest in China's stock market. By June 2015, margin loans were almost 12 percent of total Chinese stock market capitalization (3.5 percent of GDP) – surpassing the previous record for a major stock market. As a result of these and similar policies Xi's communist stock market has been extremely volatile, prompting Party intervention to stabilize prices for investors' benefit. Specifically, China's stock market surged between the Junes of 2014 and 2015 and then crashed in June 2015, August 2015, and December 2016. Xi's government took extreme measures to stop these crashes even threatening to arrest and prosecute reporters who said things that could lead to a renewed selling of stocks (see Jonathan Leightner, *Ethics, Efficiency,*

and Macroeconomics in China from Mao to Xi (Oxon, Routledge Press, 2017) chapter 11 for more details). It is as if Xi had forgotten the 2007-2008 Shanghai stock market crash in which it had lost 72 percent of its value (eliminating US$ 3.5 trillion in wealth) when he so easily encouraged the Chinese masses to invest in the "Anchor of the Chinese Dream," i.e. China's stock market. When it was booming, China's stock market was even called "the Uncle Xi bull market."

132 Xinhua News (China's official news Agency) claims Xi's "Tigers and Flies" campaign is proof that Xi Jinping is imposing the rule of law on everyone.

133 "Robber Barons, Beware: A Crackdown on Corruption Has Spread Anxiety among China's Business Elite," *Economist*, October 24, 2015. http://www.economist.com/news/china/21676814-crackdown-corruption-has-spread-anxiety-among-chinas-business-elite-robber-barons-beware

134 More than one million officials in China have been punished for corruption between 2012 and 2016 under Xi's anti-corruption drive named "Tigers and Flies." Liu Zhijun was one of the first high Chinese government officials (a "tiger") investigated under Xi's "Tigers and Flies" drive. Liu Zhijun, was China's railroad minister under Hu Jintao and Xi's government found him guilty of helping 11 people get profitable contracts or promotions and of accepting bribes. Liu had 350 apartments, 16 cars, and 18 mistresses including nurses, actresses, and train stewards. During the Deng Xiaoping, Jiang Zemin, and Hu Jintao administrations, corruption charges were never filed against a current member or past member of the Standing Committee of China's Politburo. However, Xi Jinping prosecuted Zhou Yongkang, a member of this committee under Hu Jintao. Zhou was found guilty of personally accepting bribes in excess of US$ 118,000 and taking official actions that contributed to his son and wife accruing over US$ 300 million in assets. More than thirty former or current generals have been caught, including two former vice chairmen of the Central Military Commission. In addition, fifty senior managers at SOEs were fired due to corruption in 2013 and 2014.

However, Xi's response to the Panama Papers clearly shows that Xi is not applying the rule of law to everyone equally in China. Offshore shell corporations are often, but not always, involved in corruption. When the Panama Papers accused Xi's brother-in-law, Deng Jiagui, of having two offshore shell corporations, Xi's government (instead of providing an ethical and legal purpose for these shell corporations) eliminated all reporting of these shell corporations on China's news media and internet. Xi's brother-in-law was not the only one protected by this censorship. The Panama Papers revealed that family members of seven former or current members of China's Politburo Standing Committee have offshore shell corporations. For more information see Jonathan Leightner, *Ethics, Efficiency, and Macroeconomics in China from Mao to Xi* (Oxon, Routledge Press, 2017) chapter 11.

135 The concept of a colored market is systematically examined in Katsenelinboigen, "Colored Markets in the Soviet Union," 62–85. The enlarged version of this article is published in *Internal Contradiction in the USSR*, no. 2, 1982, Chalidze Publications, 54–132 (in Russian).

136 Marx, *Economic and Philosophical Manuscripts of 1844*.

137 It can be proven mathematically that if planning is perfect, Golden Communism can be achieved without markets. This however is utopian thinking. Perfect planning or even nearly perfect planning is impossible. See Rosefielde and Pfouts, *Inclusive Economic Theory*.

138 Heller, *Catch-22*. Catch-22 offers a prosaic example of Marx's paradox by building a plot around a "double bind." Airmen mentally unfit to fly did not have to do so, but could not actually be excused. People who are crazy are not obliged to fly missions,

but anyone who applied to stop flying was showing a rational concern for his safety and was, therefore, sane and had to fly.

139 The concept of communism is plural, not singular, and there is no agreement among communists about central and peripheral doctrines. The Chinese Communist Party has been riven by doctrinal disputes, but has consistently made a few claims.

A. Epistemological Infallibilism
    The Chinese Communist Party insists that:
    1. It knows what is best for workers, peasants and other worthy social elements (minorities, genders, ethnicities). This justifies its workers' and peasants' dictatorship.
    2. It knows best how to produce and supply the people's needs in planned, market and mixed systems.
    3. It knows best how to create harmonious, enlightened, prosperous and ideally fulfilling existences for workers, peasants and other worthy social elements (minorities, genders, ethnicities).
    4. It knows best how to adapt to changing realities.
    5. It knows that other systems are inferior because capitalists, aristocrats and other classes are blinded by self-seeking. Only people's communism is trustworthy.
    These claims are tautological and therefore cannot be scientifically substantiated.

B. Ontological Infallibilism
    The Chinese Communist Party contends that:
    1. Socializing property obviates the need for private markets.
    2. Criminalizing private property prevents the exploitation of man by man.
    3. Eliminating the exploitation of man by man liberates human energy and creativity assuring complete abundance after a brief transition period.
    4. Criminalizing private property assures that workers, peasants and other worthy social elements (minorities, genders, ethnicities) achieve their full human potential because reason and sensibilities are no longer warped or constrained.
    5. Criminalizing private property assures communist harmony because liberated people are mutually supporting (communist solidarity).
    6. Criminalizing markets and entrepreneurship together with communist planning, administration and incorruptible regulation protects the people from wolves in sheep's clothing (no moral hazard because post-transition period communists are angels).
    7. Other systems are inferior because capitalists, aristocrats and other classes are bedeviled by self-seeking. Only people's communism provides full abundance and harmony.
    These claims are tautological and therefore cannot be scientifically substantiated.
    Communism's behavioral constraints are:
    1. Prohibition of private income, rent and capital gains generating property (Imposition of state ownership of the means of production; ownership of property for household consumption is permitted).
    2. Prohibition of private real estate, production and commercial markets (Imposition of state planning, production, requisitioning, rationing, administration, control and regulation).
    3. Prohibition of entrepreneurship in state-owned enterprises (Imposition of state command, control and regulation).

4.   Prohibition of private financial activities, including stock and bond markets, insurance and foreign trade (imposition of state command, control and regulation).

5.   Prohibition of rival political parties (and therefore competitive multiparty elections).

6.   Prohibition of non-communist civic organizations (criminalization, or imposition of comprehensive control and regulation).

7.   Prohibition of non-communist institutions (criminalization, or imposition of comprehensive control and regulation).

8.   Prohibition of spiritual or dualist beliefs that conflict with the dogma of dialectical materialism.

9.   Prohibition of free movement, speech and thought (Everyone must adhere to the Communist Party line).

10.   Prohibition of exploitive sexual, spiritual and parasitic practices that diminish the people's welfare and cause disharmony.

140   Especially if excess deaths are factored into the calculus. See Rosefielde, *Red Holocaust*.
141   Piketty, *The Economics of Inequality*.
142   Bergson, "Social Choice and Welfare Economics under Representative Government," 171–90; Rosefielde and Pfouts, *Inclusive Economic Theory*.
143   David Boaz, "The Man Who Told the Truth: Robert Heilbroner fessed up to the failure of socialism", January 21, 2005. http://reason.com/archives/2005/01/21/the-man-who-told-the-truth Boaz quotes Heilboner's New Yorker articles, "Less than 75 years after it officially began, the contest between capitalism and socialism is over: capitalism has won ... Capitalism organizes the material affairs of humankind more satisfactorily than socialism." Cf. Fukuyama, *The End of History and the Last Man Standing*.
144   Bergson, "Socialist Economics," 412–48; Bergson, "Socialist Calculation: A Further Word," 237–42; Bergson, "Market Socialism Revisited," 655–73; Bergson, "The USSR Before the Fall: How Poor and Why?," 29–44.
145   These claims assume in the conventional way that people everywhere are basically the same. This makes it possible to assess how institutional, moral and cultural factors might cause outcomes to differ.
146   Pareto efficiency or Pareto optimality is a state of allocation of resources further from which it is impossible to make any one individual better off without making at least one individual worse off. The concept was pioneered by Vilfredo Pareto (1848–1923). He was an Italian engineer and economist who used the concept in his studies of economic efficiency and income distribution. It has applications in academic fields such as economics, engineering and the life sciences. Pareto succeeded Léon Walras to the chair of Political Economy at the University of Lausanne in 1893. Cf. Arrow, *Social Choice and individual Values*.
147   Rosefielde and Pfouts, *Inclusive Economic Theory*.
148   The Communist Party has the right and duty to modify permissible individual behavior for the common good. For example, it may choose to an "ideal" non-generally competitive workday, communist compatible technologies and its own notion of optimal tax transfers.
149   The economy produces two composite goods. The sum of composite goods (for example, aggregate consumption and investment) by definition is GDP. $Y = C + I$.
150   Oscar Lange made this point eighty years ago. See Lange, "On the Economic Theory of Socialism I," 53–71; Lange, "On the Economic Theory of Socialism II," 123–42;

Lange, *On the Economic Theory of Socialism*; Lange, "Economics of Socialism," 299–303; Rosefielde, "Some Observations on the Concept of 'Socialism' in Contemporary Economic Theory," 229–43.

151 Leasehold property is a restricted form of control. Leaseholds are not forever. Producers only have temporary rights to use assets, preventing complete profit maximization. People in the Pareto model are permitted to consider the impact of their actions on others, but do not have to defer to the demands of others. Pink Communism implies that citizens defer to the community's will.

152 If individuals voluntarily acquiesce to society's preferences, then the competitive Pareto and Pink communist ideals are identical. Otherwise, the Pink Communist ideal point will be located at a different point along the production possibilities frontier.

153 The geometry will vary in its particulars for White and Red Communist economies.

154 Point R could be on the production possibility frontier, if perfect planning were achievable. Computopia however is unattainable. See Neuberger, "Libermanism, Computopia, and Visible Hand: The Question of Informational Efficiency," 131–44.

155 Rosefielde and Pfouts, *Inclusive Economic Theory*. Pink Communist Pareto optimality is unattainable because it violates 20 fundamental axioms of rationality. The 20 violated rationality axioms are:

1. Consumers possess well-defined continuous preferences.
2. Consumer preferences are interpersonally independent.
3. Consumers rationally select.
4. Consumers exhaustively utility search (optimizing rather than satisficing).
5. Consumers autonomously choose (individuals and households).
6. Consumers act ethically (competitively) with the framework of a Lockean social contract.
7. Well-being is solely determined by successive rational marginal choices.
8. Consumer preferences are formed rationally.
9. Production and cost functions are continuous, twice differentiable and monotonic.
10. Suppliers have complete knowledge of demand and intermediate input acquisition possibilities.
11. Suppliers possess well-defined continuous preferences that enable them to optimize with discrete production and cost functions, as well as restricted information on intermediate input supplies and demand.
12. Supplier (manager) preferences are interpersonally independent.
13. Managers rationally select.
14. Managers exhaustively search profit and cost minimization possibilities (optimizing rather than satisficing).
15. Managers autonomously choose (CEOs and collective corporate decision makers).
16. Managers act ethically (competitively) within the framework of a Lockean social contract.
17. Managers' preferences are formed rationally.
18. Economic institutions are comprehensively rationally designed.
19. Macroeconomic theory is complete and uniquely determinative.
20. Politicians and voters are comprehensively rational actors free from moral hazard.

This means that point E is a pipedream both for White, Red and Pink Communist regimes. The problem arises because reason is "bounded." Workers, owners, managers consumers and public authorities cannot know all the things that optimal rational economic theory requires.

The deficiency has been recognized for more than half a century and addressed in the West by reworking Paretian principles in a bounded rational, fuzzy set framework to show that while the best is unattainable, competitive and/or counterpart computational systems are capable of yielding satisfactory results. Simon, "A Behavioral Model of Rational Choice," 99–118; Simon, *Models of Man: Social and Rational-Mathematical Essays on Rational Human Behavior in a Social Setting*; Simon. "Theories of Decision Making in Economic Behavioral Science," 99–118; Simon, *Models of Bounded Rationality*.

Firms cannot completely maximize profits, and may exert monopoly power in bounded rational reality. Consumers cannot completely maximize utility and governmental authorities cannot devise reliable cost-benefit tests to make optimal public choices. Everyone has to accept that the best isn't ascertainable in any economic system, but this doesn't mean that all systems are equally deficient. Xi's communism is intrinsically superior to Mao's anti-competitive bounded rational "best" because it imposes stringent constraints on property rights, democracy and personal liberty. This claim is easily confirmed by the bounded rational, "fuzzy set" circles drawn around key equilibrium and disequilibrium points in Figure 6.1, and the production frontiers in Figure 6.2. White Communist point E is transformed into a range, but still surpasses counterpart Red Communists, ceteris paribus.

The same line of argument holds for a wide range of cultural, civic, communitarian, social, ethical, psychological, spiritual and religious variables excluded by the rationality requirements of optimal and bounded rational neoclassical economy theory.

156   Rosefielde and Pfouts, *Inclusive Economic Theory*. In mathematics, fuzzy sets are sets whose elements have degrees of membership. Seising, "The Fuzzification of Systems. The Genesis of Fuzzy Set Theory and Its Initial Applications—Developments up to the 1970s"; Simon, "A Behavioral Model of Rational Choice," 99–118; Simon, *Models of Man: Social and Rational-Mathematical Essays on Rational Human Behavior in a Social Setting*; Simon, *"Theories of Decision Making in Economic Behavioral Science," 99–118*; Simon, *Models of Bounded Rationality*.

157   Pink Communism does not have to be evaluated using the individualist benchmark. Figures 6.1 and 6.2 can be constructed starting with ideal social conscious individuals. This makes point E the Pareto-efficient Pink Communist benchmark that is used to evaluate technically and economically inefficient points.

158   Samuelson, *Foundations of Economic Analysis*, Chapter 8; Samuelson, "Evaluation of Real National Income, 1–29; Samuelson, "Social Indifference Curves," *Quarterly Journal of Economics*, 1–22; Bator, "The Simple Analytics of Welfare Maximization," 22–59; van de Graaf, *Theoretical Welfare Economics*.

159   The democratic competitive ideal can accommodate compassionate transfers of income and wealth through private charity or by empowering the government to serve as transfer agent. The Pareto equilibrium points in Figures 6.1–6.4 will vary with these income and wealth transfers, but as before all will be achieved with the assistance of Walrasian and Marshallian automatic price and quantity adjustment mechanisms. Voluntary compassionate transfers thus allow ideal democratic competitive systems to be as egalitarian or inegalitarian as citizens' desire.

160   Well-being is most commonly used in philosophy to describe what is non-instrumentally or ultimately good for a person. Griffin, *Well-being*; Seligman,

Flourish: A New Understanding of Happiness and Well-being—And How to Achieve Them; Kahneman, Diener and Schwarz, eds, *Well-being: The Foundations of Hedonic Psychology.*

161 Satisfaction, fulfillment and contentment depend on a host of psychological, psychiatric, physiological spiritual and ethical factors including individual concerns about inequality.

162 Well-being also takes account of psychological gains or losses experienced from market volatility, economic insecurity, adversarial social relations and market-related corruption.

163 Bergson, "A Reformulation of Certain Aspects of Welfare Economics," 210–34. Bergson, *Essays in Normative Economics.* Sen, "Personal Utilities and Public Judgements: Or What's Wrong with Welfare Economics," 537–588.

164 Dantzig, *Linear Programming and Extensions* Weitzman, "Prices versus Quantities," 477–91. Harrison, "Command and Collapse: The Fundament Problem of Command in a Partially Centralized Economy," 296–314.

165 Williamson, *Markets and Hierarchies*; Weitzman, "The New Soviet Incentive Model," 251–257. Ross, "The Economic Theory of Agency: The Principal's Problem," 134–139. Maskin and Tirole, "The Principal-Agent Relationship with an Informed Principal, I: Private Values," 379–410; Maskin and Tirole, "The Principal-Agent Relationship with an Informed Principal, II: Common Values," 1–42; Lewis and Sappington, "Ignorance in Agency Problems," 169–183; Laffont and Tirole, *A Theory of Incentives in Procurement and Regulation;* Berliner, *Innovation in Soviet Industry*; North, *Understanding the Process of Economic Change*; Ostrom, *Understanding Institutional Diversity*; Williamson, *The Economic Institutions of Capitalism: Firms, Markets and Relational Contracting;* Williamson, *Mechanisms of Governance*; Williamson, "The New Institutional Economics: Taking Stock, Looking Ahead," 595–613. Also see Coase, "The New Institutional Economics," 72–4; McCloskey, *The Bourgeois Era.*

166 Rosefielde and Pfouts, *Inclusive Economic Theory.*

167 Macroeconomic phenomenon like involuntary unemployment, financial crises, and inflation are not considered here because they can arise in any Pink Communist system regardless of hue. Cf. Shiller, *Irrational Exuberance*; Greenspan, "Never Saw it Coming," November/December 2013, where he claims that he disregarded "animal spirits" in 2008, despite his own warnings about "irrational exuberance," http://www.foreignaffairs.com/articles/140161/alan-greenspan/never-saw-it-coming. See also Krugman, *The Return of Depression Economics and the Crisis of 2008.*

168 Le Grand, "Equity versus Efficiency: The Elusive Trade-Off," 554–568; Okun, *Equality and Efficiency: The Big Tradeoff.*

169 Darden, *Economic Liberalism and Its Rivals.*

170 Smith, *The Wealth of Nations*; Locke, *Second Treatise of Government*, 1689. http://www.earlymoderntexts.com/assets/pdfs/locke1689a.pdf

171 Rosefielde, *Soviet International Trade in Heckscher-Ohlin Perspective*; Rosefielde, "Factor Proportions and Economic Rationality in Soviet International Trade 1955–1968," 670–81.

172 James Truslow Adams characterized the American Dream as "life should be better and richer and fuller for everyone, with opportunity for each according to ability or achievement" regardless of social class or circumstances of birth. http://www.loc.gov/teachers/classroommaterials/lessons/american-dream/students/thedream.html

173 Arrow, "A Difficulty in the Concept of Social Welfare," 328–46; Arrow, *Social Choice and Individual Values.* Arrow's demonstration that balloting doesn't provide faithful democratic representatives with sufficient information to always act in accordance with the majority's will is commonly referred to as Arrow's "impossibility theorem," or "Arrow's

paradox." Suzumura, Arrow and Sen, eds., *Handbook of Social Choice and Welfare*. The theorem states that when voters have three or more distinct alternatives, no rank order voting system can convert the ranked preferences of individuals into a community-wide (complete and transitive) ranking while also meeting the criteria of unrestricted domain, non-dictatorship, Pareto efficiency and interdependence of irrelevant alternatives. There are problems with Arrow's numerical demonstration. See Eric Maskin's introduction in Arrow, *Social Choice and Individual Values*. The author does not accept the adequacy of Arrow's proof.

174 The democratic component of real Liberal Democracy as the term liberal requires does not choose sides. It represents all of the people. Rosefielde and Mills, *Democracy and Its Elected Enemies*.

175 Rosefielde, *Trump's Populist America*.

176 Trump supports Social Security, Medicare and Medicaid.

177 Maciej Kislowski defines Liberal Democracy as a system that tries to please everyone, and Illiberal Democracy as one where state power is used to favor specific groups. The Obama administration ruled in the interest of Wall Street and diverse social activists instead of all the people, and hence was illiberal. Kisilowski, "How Eastern Europe Blew Up the West," https://www.project-syndicate.org/onpoint/how-eastern-europe-blew-up-the-west-by-maciej-kisilowski-2017-01?utm_source=Project+Syndicate+Newsletter&utm_campaign=588ae6c414-. "Like many disruptive products and popular brands, illiberal democracy does not try to please everyone; rather, it targets a carefully selected segment of "voter-customers," and gives them exactly what they want."

178 The term "Illiberal Democracy" has become part of the contemporary lexicon, but most analysts use is pejoratively to stigmatize populist electoral systems. The idea is that those who disagree with "progressives" including the working class and populist majority are "deplorables." See Kisilowski, "How Eastern Europe Blew Up the West." https://www.project-syndicate.org/onpoint/how-eastern-europe-blew-up-the-west-by-maciej-kisilowski-2017-01?utm_source=Project+Syndicate+Newsletter&utm_campaign=588ae6c414-. "When Hillary Clinton called Trump's supporters a 'basket of deplorables,' she quite accurately described one segment of the political market that Orbán's innovation targets. But the illiberal democrat speaks not only to reactionaries eager to restore traditional social hierarchies, but also to working-class voters fearful of unemployment and downward mobility. The rest of society – ethnic, religious, and ideological minorities, including the urban 'creative class' – then forms the opposition. Illiberal democracy subverts the idea – held by European social democrats and American Democrats since the 1960s – that working-class and minority voters should forge a progressive alliance to counter conservatives. Intellectually, such a 'stronger together' alliance makes sense; but it has three major flaws that Orbán and Kaczyński have exploited. First, the economic interests of white (or native) working-class voters and those of minorities are often not aligned, because they are competing with one another for jobs and social benefits. This is especially true when slow growth turns the division of the economic pie into a zero-sum game. When funds are limited, should the Hungarian government spend money on educating Roma children, or on retraining displaced ethnic Hungarian workers? Second, working-class voters often adhere to traditional conservative values. While a farmer in Eastern Poland or a factory worker in Michigan might be persuaded to support gay rights or women's empowerment in exchange for economic redistribution, working-class voters have not supported such causes in large numbers. Illiberal democracy is effective because it disentangles desired goods from unwanted add-ons, which is the essence of modern business innovation.

Just as Airbnb allows us to find lodging without unnecessary hotel frills, illiberal democrats offer working-class voters economic help with no civil-rights strings attached. Third, in many electorates, members of a social majority seem to value vilification of minorities as an intrinsic good, irrespective of wealth transfers. And as Yale University's Amy Chua and others have shown, targeting minorities can be a highly effective tool for political mobilization."

179   This is a basic problem in welfare economics. Abram Bergson proved long ago that judgments about systems merit are subjective. There is no single subjective best. People can have strong opinions, but they cannot stop others from disagreeing. See Bergson, "A Reformulation of Certain Aspects of Welfare Economics," 210–34; Bergson, *Essays in Normative Economics*; Sen, "Personal Utilities and Public Judgements: Or What's Wrong with Welfare Economics," 537–88.

180   The litmus test for Liberal Democracy is not the level of economic activity; it is consumer sovereignty in the private sector and electoral sovereignty over public goods. If some individuals and/or governments improperly infringe citizens' property and civic rights, democratic market systems degenerate into Illiberal Democracies even if all business goes global.

181   Stiglitz, *Globalization and Its Discontents*; Stiglitz, *Making Globalization Work*.

182   Rosefielde, Kuboniwa, Mizobata and Haba, eds., *The Unwinding of the Globalist Dream*.

183   Liberal Democratic nations can enter into international agreements and create transnational agencies to promote their common good without altering their liberal character. However, if these agreements and transnational agencies improperly infringe citizens' property and civic rights, the global system will become illiberal.

184   For a discussion of the concept see Talbott, "America Abroad: The Birth of the Global Nation," http://channelingreality.com/Documents/1992_Strobe_Talbot_Global_Nation.pdf. "I'll bet that within the next hundred years (I'm giving the world time for setbacks and myself time to be out of the betting game, just in case I lose this one), nationhood as we know it will be obsolete; all states will recognize a single, global authority. A phrase briefly fashionable in the mid-20th century – "citizen of the world" – will have assumed real meaning by the end of the 21st." "The best mechanism for democracy, whether at the level of the multinational state or that of the planet as a whole, is not an all-powerful Leviathan or centralized superstate, but a federation, a union of separate states that allocate certain powers to a central government while retaining many others for themselves. Federalism has already proved the most successful of all political experiments, and organizations like the World Federalist Association have for decades advocated it as the basis for global government. Federalism is largely an American invention. For all its troubles, including its own serious bout of secessionism 130 years ago and the persistence of various forms of tribalism today, the US is still the best example of a multinational federal state. If that model does indeed work globally, it would be the logical extension of the Founding Fathers' wisdom, therefore a special source of pride for a world government's American constituents. Cf. https://www.pri.org/verticals/global-nation (this is a global nation advocacy group); Goldberg, "America: Indispensable Nation, or Indispensable Partner?," http://www.realclearworld.com/articles/2016/10/12/america_indispensable_nation_or_indispensable_partner_112087.html. "America and its global role have been redefined during those 18 years; we are no longer the indispensable nation, we are the indispensable partner, and there is a big philosophical difference between those two ideas. The indispensable nation – like the individual entrepreneur, i.e. Donald Trump – takes independent risks to protect its own status. The indispensable partner leads and takes

risks to protect the stability of its network – the new joint ventured world – and to grow that network."

185 Globalism's principal illiberal features are said to be abetting Wall Street's financial domination, imposing western big business friendly laws and regulations, enhancing predatory western penetration into Third World markets, and pressing social justice causes that transgress non-western cultural preferences.

186 Globalizers believe that transnational institutions provide a global infrastructure that enhances the productivity of foreign trade and allows leaders to reap the lion's share of the profits.

187 Denyer, "As Trump Prepares for Office, Concerns about China Trade Intensify," https://www.washingtonpost.com/world/asia_pacific/as-trump-prepares-for-office-concerns-about-china-trade-reach-a-crescendo/2016/11/27/472b5c26-b199-11e6-bc2d-19b3d759cfe7_story.html.

188 Fidler, Chen and Wei, "China's Xi Jinping Seizes Role as Leader on Globalization," https://www.wsj.com/articles/chinas-xi-jinping-defends-globalization-1484654899.

189 Van Ness, "Does China have What It Takes to Become a Global Hegemon?," http://wilsonquarterly.com/quarterly/the-post-obama-world/does-china-have-what-it-takes-to-become-a-global-hegemon/.

190 This would be a fresh twist on the Communist Party of the Soviet Union's (CPSU) over-lordship of the Communist International (Comintern). Lenin leveraged his authority over the CPSU by making it primus inter pares in the communist world. Xi could outdo Lenin by having the CPC set the rules not just for the communist world, but the entire contemporary global order. The Communist International, abbreviated as Comintern, and also known as the Third International (1919–1943), was an international communist organization that advocated world communism. The International intended to fight "by all available means, including armed force, for the overthrow of the international bourgeoisie and for the creation of an international Soviet republic as a transition stage to the complete abolition of the State."

The Comintern was founded after the 1915 Zimmerwald Conference in which Vladimir Lenin had organized the "Zimmerwald Left" against those who refused to approve any statement explicitly endorsing socialist revolutionary action, and after the 1916 dissolution of the Second International (http://spartacus-educational.com/RUScomintern.htm).

191 Tom Miles and Stephanie Nebehay, "Xi portrays China as global leader as Trump era looms", *Reuters*, January 18, 2017 (http://www.reuters.com/article/us-china-usa-idUSKBN1522OS). "China will build a "new model" of relations with the United States, President Xi Jinping said on Wednesday in a speech that portrayed China as the leader of a globalized world where only international cooperation could solve the big problems. 'We will strive to build a new model of major country relations with the United States, a comprehensive strategic partnership of coordination with Russia, a partnership for peace, growth, reform and among different civilizations and a partnership of unity and cooperation with BRICS countries.'"

192 This is an ancient problem. The furies (Erinyes, or Eumenides) were infernal deities of vengeance who relentlessly hounded sinners oblivious to the collateral damage. They were the red guards and jihadists of the Greco-Roman pantheon. Their motives were righteous, but the consequences were pernicious to the greater good.

193 Rosefielde and Mills, *Democracy and Its Elected Enemies.*

194 Petrov, *From Managed Democracy to Sovereign Democracy: Putin's Regime Evolution in 2005.* https://www2.gwu.edu/~ieresgwu/assets/docs/ponars/pm_0396.pdf.

195 "Confucius says, Xi does," *The Economist*, July 25, 2015, http://www.economist
.com/news/china/21659753-communist-party-turns-ancient-philosophy-support-
confucius-says-xi-does.

"Though the party has quietly been rehabilitating Confucius for some time,
under Mr Xi the pace has quickened. In February 2014 he convened a "collective
study" session of the ruling Politburo at which he said that traditional culture should
act as a 'wellspring' nourishing the party's values." "Why China Is Turning Back to
Confucius," *Wall Street Journal*, September 20, 2015, http://www.wsj.com/articles/
why-china-is-turning-back-to-confucius-1442754000.

196 Confucianism is a body of moral philosophy and a strategy for harmonious, self-
regulating societal governance devised by Kong Fuzi (Confucius) (551–479 BC), elaborated in the Analects of Confucius, and the Five Classics. His aphoristic teachings
begin with the premise that good laws and fear of punishment are insufficient for
achieving social harmony. People need to be taught the wisdom of moral conduct,
and devise good laws accordingly, buttressed by ritual that inculcates a self-disciplining
sense of guilt. Veneration of sage emperors, reverence for ancestors, primacy of family, respect for elders (and husbands by wives), deference to superiors, and loyalty are
stressed over individual self-seeking, competitiveness and minority empowerment.
This is accomplished through the study of ancient precepts, self-evidently virtuous
maxims that provide proper rules of conduct subtlety tailored to suit every situation.
The best government combines Weberian functional efficiency and incorruptibility
with familial compassion. It is meritocratic, stressing moral worthiness, rather than
nepotism. Confucius, *Confucius: Analects—With Selections from Traditional Commentaries*;
Annping, *The Authentic Confucius, A Life of Thought and Politics*.

197 The absence of a theory of family demand has frequently been noted in passing
in economic literature, but there seems to be no development or extensive discussion of this subject, because interpersonal utility is income measurable. For example,
Samuelson mused about the issue: "… what is a man? Or a consumer? I am not so
much concerned with the problem of Dr. Jekyll and Mr. Hyde but with the problem of
Dr. Jekyll and Mrs. Jekyll. Much consumption behavior is family rather than individual
behavior. Now a family must be quite sophisticated indeed to end up with a consistent
set of collective preferences: e.g. if they set up the rule that the wife will always spend
99 percent (or 50 percent) of the income on her needs and the husband 1 percent
(or 50 percent) on his quite different needs, this will not be consistent with an inte-
grable set of price ratio elements. Only if the family acts in terms of a Bergson Social
Welfare Function will this condition result. But to explain this further would take me
into the frontier of research in welfare economics" (Samuelson's emphasis). Samuelson,
"The Problem of Integrability in Utility Theory," 255–85.

198 Rosefielde and Pfouts, *Inclusive Economic Theory*.

199 Qin Shi Huang Di was China's first emperor. He was a "legalist" despot and sworn
enemy of Confucianism. Qin was the clan name of the royal house of the State of Qin.
Shi is first. Huang refers to Three August Ones who ruled at the dawn of Chinese
history, and Di is the legendary Five Di (Sovereigns) who ruled immediately after the
Three Huang. After his death in 210 BC the Qin Empire collapsed, but was reconsti-
tuted under the first Han emperor in 202 BC. For clarity he is best and most simply
called Qin Shi Huang (First Emperor of Qin). His personal name was Ying Zheng,
King of the Chinese State of Qin (247–221 BC). Qin Shi Huang was an aspiring
totalitarian, acting in accordance with the legalist principles of his Prime Minister Li
Si. Although he was neither omniscient nor omnipotent, he sought insofar as humanly
possible with the technologies of the day to nano-direct his subjects' lives in this world,

and the next. He commanded his ministers and their staffs to execute his political, economic and civic instructions and draconian laws. Under this scheme there was no scope for independent authority above his own (although there was wiggle room created by the ambiguities and the restricted scope of the laws) including anything that might be construed as common law or Confucian precepts (Confucianism was banned), an attitude that may well have extended to the gods.

200 Legalism, literally "School of Law," was one of the main philosophic currents during the Warring States Period. Legalism was one of four main philosophical schools during the Spring and Autumn Period (722–481 BC), and the period of the Warring States(450?-221 BC). It was pragmatic and utilitarian. The school's most famous proponent, Han Fei Zi, believed that a ruler should use the following three tools to govern his subjects: (1) Fa, the law code must be clearly written and made public. All people under the ruler were equal before the law. Laws should reward those who obey them and punish those who break them. Rewards and punishments are predictable. The system of law, not the ruler's edict, governed the state. If the law is successfully enforced, even a weak ruler will be strong. (2) Shu, special tactics and "secrets" protected the ruler from insurrections. Rulers had to be enigmatic to deter intrigue. (3) Shi, it is the position of the ruler, not the ruler himself or herself, that holds the power.

201 Olson and Edwards, eds., *The Encyclopedia of Philosophy*. Deontological ethics, or deontology (from the Greek *deon*, "obligation, duty," and *logia*) judges the morality of an action based on the action's adherence to a rule or rules. It is sometimes described as "duty" or "obligation" or "rule"-based ethics, because rules "bind you to your duty." Deontological ethics is commonly contrasted to consequentialism. Deontological ethics is also contrasted to pragmatic ethics.

202 Scheffler, *The Rejection of Consequentialism: A Philosophical Investigation of the Considerations Underlying Rival Moral Conceptions*; Portmore, *Commonsense Consequentialism: Wherein Morality Meets Rationality*.

203 The "silver rule" is a variant on the Christian "golden rule": "never impose on others what you would not choose for yourself" (Analects XV, 24). Confucius, *Confucius: Analects – with Selections from Traditional Commentaries*.

204 Allen, *Plato: The Republic*.

205 Chan, *Chu Hsi and Neo-Confucianism*.

206 Fung, *A History of Chinese Philosophy*; Rozman, ed., *The East Asian Region: Confucian Heritage and Its Modern Adaption*; Wright, *Confucianism and Chinese Civilization*.

207 More, *Utopia*, 1516.

208 https://www.transparency.org/cpi2015/. The index scores were Denmark 91, Singapore 85, Hong Kong 75, Taiwan 62, China 37, and Sudan 12.

209 Esping-Andersen, *Social Foundations of Postindustrial Economies*.

210 Taiwan, Singapore, Hong Kong and South Korea are frequently described as Asian tigers, or little dragons, to stress their economic vibrance (1960–1990). See Kinzley, *Industrial Harmony in Modern Japan: The Invention of a Tradition*.

211 Taiwan not only benefited from inexpensive factors of production (including labor), easy access to American and Japanese markets, and technology transfer, but the traditional Confucian reverence for education swiftly became a vehicle for steadily elevating productive skills. Foreign demand disciplined Taiwanese suppliers to produce goods with desirable characteristics. Technology transfer raised factor productivity, while authoritarianism repressed trade unions, and Confucian ethics facilitated cooperative labor-management relations and cost efficiency. Like Deng Xiaoping's subsequent market liberalization on the mainland, Chiang's authoritarian modernization program was bolstered further by the advantages of relative economic backwardness. Microeconomic

inefficiencies associated with Confucian restrictions on individualism were more than offset by climbing the value-added ladder from a low to a high productivity regime.

212 Social welfare expenditures as GDP shares in 2002 were Japan 18.4, America 11.9, South Korea 5.5, Germany 28.4, Taiwan 4.9, France 28.6, Singapore 1.8, UK 22.4, China 0.3. *Source*: See Gordon.

213 Yu-Chen Lan, "The Politics of Taiwanese Welfare State Transformation: Postindustrial Pressures, Regime Shifts and Social Policy Responses in the 1990s and Beyond."

214 Tsang, *The Vitality of Taiwan: Politics, Economics, Society and Culture.*

215 Rosefielde and Liu, "Sovereign Debt Crises: Solidarity and Power."

216 Bentham believed utility could be measured by some complex introspective examination and that it should guide the design of social policies and laws. Stigler, "The Development of Utility Theory," 307–27.

217 Bergson, "Social Choice and Welfare Economics under Representative Government," 171–90.

BIBLIOGRAPHY

Allen, Reginald. *Plato: The Republic*. New Haven, CT: Yale University Press, 2006.

Arrow, Kenneth. "A Difficulty in the Concept of Social Welfare." *Journal of Political Economy* 58, no. 4 (August 1950): 328–46.

———. *Social Choice and Individual Values*. New York: Wiley, 1951.

———. *Social Choice and Individual Values*. Princeton, NJ: Princeton University Press, 2012.

Auslin, Michael. *The End of the Asian Century*. New Haven, CT: Yale University Press, 2017.

Bator, Francis. "The Simple Analytics of Welfare Maximization." *American Economic Review* 47, no. 1 (March 1957): 22–59.

Becker, Gary S. *The Economic Approach to Human Behavior*. Chicago, IL: University of Chicago Press, 1976.

Bergson, Abram. "A Reformulation of Certain Aspects of Welfare Economics." *Quarterly Journal of Economics* 52, no. 2 (February 1938): 310–34.

———. *The Economics of Soviet Planning*. New Haven, CT: Yale University Press, 1964.

———. *Essays in Normative Economics*. Cambridge, MA: Belknap Press, 1966.

———. "Market Socialism Revisited." *Journal of Political Economy* 75, no. 4 (October 1967): 655–73.

———. "Social Choice and Welfare Economics under Representative Government." *Journal of Public Economics* 6, no. 3 (October 1976): 171–90.

———. "Socialist Calculation: A Further Word." In *Essays in Normative Economics*, edited by Bergson, Abram 237–42. Cambridge, MA: Belknap Press, 1966.

———. "Socialist Economics." In *A Survey of Contemporary Economics*, edited by Howard Sylvester Ellis, 412–48. Homewood, IL: Richard D. Irwin, 1948.

———. "The USSR before the Fall: How Poor and Why?" *Journal of Economic Perspectives* 5, no. 4 (Fall 1991): 29–44.

Berliner Joseph. *Factory and Manager in the USSR*. Cambridge, MA: Harvard University Press, 1957.

———. *The Innovation Decision in Soviet Industry*. Cambridge, MA: MIT Press, 1976.

Boaz, David. "The Man Who Told the Truth: Robert Heilbroner Fessed Up to the Failure Of Socialism," January 21, 2005. http://reason.com/archives/2005/01/21/the-man-who-told-the-truth.

Chan, Wing-tsit. *Chu Hsi and Neo-Confucianism*. Honolulu, HI: University of Hawaii Press, 1986.

Chang, Jung, and Jon Halliday. *Mao: The Unknown Story*. New York: Anchor, 2006.

Chin, Annping. *The Authentic Confucius, A Life of Thought and Politics.* New York: Scribner, 2007.

Coase, Ronald. "The New Institutional Economics." *American Economic Review* 88, no. 2 (May 1998): 72–4.

———. "The Problem of Social Cost." *Journal of Law and Economics* 3 (October 1960): 1–44.

Confucius, Edward Slingerland. *Analects—With Selections from Traditional Commentaries.* Indianapolis, IN: Hackett, 2003.

Dantzig, George. *Linear Programming and Extensions.* Princeton, NJ: Princeton University Press, 1963.

Darden, Keith. *Economic Liberalism and Its Rivals.* Cambridge, MA: Cambridge University Press, 2009.

Debreu, Gérard. "Existence of Competitive Equilibrium." In *Handbook of Mathematical Economics, Handbook of Economics Series,* edited by Kenneth J. Arrow and Michael Intriligator, 697–744. Amsterdam, the Netherlands, New York: Elsevier North-Holland, 1981.

———. *The Theory of Value: An Axiomatic Analysis of Economic Equilibrium.* New York: Wiley, 1959.

Deininger, Klaus, and Jin Songqing. "Securing Property Rights in Transition: Lessons from Implementation of China's Rural Land Contracting Law." *Journal of Economic Behavior and Organization* 70, no. 1–2 (May 2009): 22–38.

Dong, Fureng. "China's Price Reform." *Cambridge Journal of Economics* 10 (1986): 291–300.

Dorfman, Robert, Paul Samuelson, and Robert Solow. *Linear Programming and Economic Analysis.* New York: McGraw-Hill, 1958.

Engels, Friedric, and Karl Marx. *The Communist Manifesto.* 1848.

Esping-Andersen, Gosta. *Social Foundations of Postindustrial Economies.* New York: Oxford University Press, 1999.

Fukuyama, Francis. *The End of History and the Last Man Standing.* New York: Avon Books, 1992.

Fung, Yu-lan. *A History of Chinese Philosophy.* Princeton, NJ: Princeton University Press, 1952–53.

Gordon, Hou-sheng Chan. "The Development of Social Welfare Policy in Taiwan: Welfare Debates between the Left and the Right." Working Paper, Doshisha University, Kyoto, Japan, January 2008.

Gorky, Maxim. *A Sky Blue Life.* 1925.

Gray, Alexander. *The Socialist Tradition: Moses to Lenin.* London: Longmans, Green and Company. 1946.

Greenspan, Alan. "Never Saw It Coming." *Foreign Affairs,* November/December 2013.

Griffin, James. *Well-being.* Oxford: Clarendon Press, 1986.

Harrison, Mark. "Command and Collapse: The Fundamental Problem of Command in a Partially Centralized Economy." *Comparative Economic Studies* 47, no. 2 (2005): 296–314.

Heilbroner, Robert. *The Worldly Philosophers.* New York: Simon & Schuster, 1953.

Heller, Joseph. *Catch-22.* New York: Simon & Schuster, 1961.

Hinton, William. "A Response to Hugh Deane." *Monthly Review* 40, no. 10 (1989): 20–1.

Hong. *Fanshen: A Documentary of Revolution in a Chinese Village.* New York: Vantage Books, 1966.

Horvat, Branko, Mihailo Marcovic, and Rudi Supek Rudi, eds. *Self-Governing Socialism.* White Plains, NY: International Arts and Sciences Press, 1975.

Hsueh, Roselyn. *China's Regulatory State: A New Strategy for Globalization.* Ithaca, NY: Cornell University Press, 2011.

Huchet, Jean-Francois, and Xavier Richet. "Between Bureaucracy and Market: Chinese Industrial Groups in Search of New Forms of Corporate Governance." Paper presented at the American Economics Meetings, New Orleans, LA., January 6, 2001.

Hughes, Neil. *China's Economic Challenge: Smashing the Iron Rice Bowl.* Armonk, NY: M.E. Sharpe, 2002.

Kahneman, Daniel. *Thinking, Fast and Slow.* New York: Farrar, Straus and Giroux, 2011.

Kahneman, Daniel, Edward Diener, and Schwarz Norbert, eds. *Well-being: The Foundations of Hedonic Psychology*. New York: Russell Sage Foundation, 1999.

Kakutani, Shizuo. "A Generalization of Brouwer's Fixed Point Theorem." *Duke Mathematical Journal* 8, no. 3 (1941): 457–9.

Kantorovich, Leonid. *The Best Uses of Economic Resources*. Oxford, NY: Pergamon, 1965.

Katsenelinboigen, Aron. "Colored Markets in the Soviet Union." *Soviet Studies* 29, no. 1 (1977): 62–85.

Kinzley, W. Dean. *Industrial Harmony in Modern Japan: The Invention of a Tradition*. London: Routledge, 1991.

Kisilowski, Maciej. "How Eastern Europe Blew Up the West." *Project Syndicate*, January 29, 2017.

Kropotkin, Peter. *Mutual Aid: A Factor of Evolution*. London: Freedom Press, 1998.

Krugman, Paul. *The Return of Depression Economics and the Crisis of 2008*. New York: W.W. Norton Company, 2009.

Kung, Lin. "The Decline of Township-and-Village Enterprises in China's Economic Transition." *World Development* 35, no. 4 (2007): 569–84.

Laffont, Jean-Jacques, and Jean Tirole. *A Theory of Incentives in Procurement and Regulation*. Cambridge, MA: MIT Press, 1993.

Lange, Oscar. "Economics of Socialism." *Journal of Political Economy* 50, no. 2 (1942): 299–303.

———. "On the Economic Theory of Socialism I." *Review of Economic Studies* 4, no. 1 (1936): 53–71.

———. "On the Economic Theory of Socialism II." *Review of Economic Studies* 4, no. 2 (1937): 123–42.

Lange, Oscar, and Fred M. Taylor. *On the Economic Theory of Socialism*. Ann Arbor, MI: University of Michigan Press, 1938.

Le Grand, Julian. "Equity versus Efficiency: The Elusive Trade-Off." *Ethics 100*, no. 3 (April 1990): 554–68.

Leightner, Jonathan. *Ethics, Efficiency, and Macroeconomics in China from Mao to Xi*. Oxon: Routledge Press, 2017.

Lewis, Tracy, and David Sappington. "Ignorance in Agency Problems." *Journal of Economic Theory* 61 (1993): 169–83.

Locke, John. *Second Treatise of Government*. 1689.

Lodge, Milton, and Charles Taber. "Three Steps toward a Theory of Motivated Political Reasoning." In *Elements of Reason: Cognition, Choice and Bounds of Rationality*, edited by Arthur Lupia. Cambridge: Cambridge University Press, 2000.

Lupia, Arthur, ed. *Elements of Reason: Cognition, Choice and Bounds of Rationality*. Cambridge: Cambridge University Press, 2000.

MacFarquhar, Roderick, and Michael Schoenhals. *Mao's Last Revolution*. Boston, MA: Belknap Harvard, 2006.

Marx, Karl. *Economic and Philosophical Manuscripts of 1844*. Moscow: Progress Publishers, 1959.

Maskin, Edward, and Jean Tirole. "The Principal-Agent Relationship with an Informed Principal, I: Private Values." *Econometrica* 58 (1990): 379–410.

———. "The Principal-Agent Relationship with an Informed Principal, II: Common Values." *Econometrica* 60 (1992): 1–42.

McCloskey, Donald. *The Bourgeois Era*. Chicago, IL: University of Chicago Press, 2010.

Meisner, Maurice. *The Deng Xiaoping Era: An Inquiry into the Fate of Chinese Socialism 1978–1994*. New York: Hill and Wang, 1996.

Meisner, Maurice. *Mao's China and After: A History of the People's Republic*. 3rd ed., 90–9. New York: The Free Press, 1999.

Nash, John. "Equilibrium Points in N-Person Games." *Proceedings of the National Academy of Sciences of the United States of America* 36, no. 1 (1950): 48–9.

Naughton, Barry. *The Chinese Economy: Transitions and Growth*. Cambridge, MA: MIT Press, 2007.

Nelson, Richard, and Sydney Winter. *An Evolutionary Theory of Economic Change*. Cambridge, MA: Harvard University Press, 1982.

Neuberger, Egon. "Libermanism, Computopia, and Visible Hand: The Question of Informational Efficiency." *American Economic Review* 56, no. 1/2 (March 1, 1966): 131–44.

Nolan, Peter. "The China Puzzle: 'Touching Stones to Cross the River.'" *Challenge* 37, no. 1 (January/February 1994): 25.

North, Douglass. *Understanding the Process of Economic Change.* Princeton, NJ: Princeton University Press, 2005.

Oi, Jean. "Fiscal Reform and the Economic Foundations of Local State Corporatism." *World Politics* 45 (1992): 99–126.

Okun, Arthur. *Equality and Efficiency: The Big Tradeoff.* Washington, DC: Brookings Institute, 2015.

Olson, Robert, and Paul Edwards, ed. *The Encyclopedia of Philosophy.* London: Collier Macmillan, 1967.

Ostrom, Elizabeth. *Understanding Institutional Diversity.* Princeton, NJ: Princeton University Press, 2005.

Petrov, Nikolai. *From Managed Democracy to Sovereign Democracy: Putin's Regime Evolution in 2005*, Phillips and Sherwood, November 17, 2015.

Piketty, Thomas. *Capital in the Twenty-First Century.* Cambridge, MA: Belknap Press, 2014.

———. *The Economics of Inequality*, 291–300. The Belknap Press of Harvard University Press, Cambridge: 2015.

Ponars Policy Memo no. 396 (December 2005).

Portmore, Douglas. *Commonsense Consequentialism: Wherein Morality Meets Rationality.* New York: Oxford University Press, 2011.

Rosefielde, Steven. *Asian Economic Systems.* Singapore: World Scientific Publishers, 2013.

———. "Factor Proportions and Economic Rationality in Soviet International Trade 1955–1968." *American Economic Review* 64, no. 4 (September 1974): 670–81.

———. "The Illusion of Westernization in Russia and China." *Comparative Economic Studies* 49 (2007): 495–513.

———. *Red Holocaust.* London: Routledge, 2010.

———. *Russian Economy from Lenin to Putin.* New York, Wiley, 2007.

———. "Some Observations on the Concept of 'Socialism' in Contemporary Economic Theory." *Soviet Studies* 25, no. 2 (1973): 229–43.

———. *Soviet International Trade in Heckscher-Ohlin Perspective.* Waltham, MA: Heath-Lexington, August 1973.

———. *Trump's Populist America.* Singapore: World Scientific Publishers, 2017.

———., ed. *World Communism at the Crossroads: Military Ascendancy, Political Economy, and Human Welfare*, 260–73. Boston, MA: Martinus Nijhoff Publishers, 1980.

Rosefielde, Steven, and Henry Latane. "Decentralized Economic Control in the Soviet Union and Maoist China: One-Man Rule versus Collective Self-Management," In *World Communism at the Crossroads: Military Ascendancy, Political Economy, and Human Welfare*, edited by Steven Rosefielde, 260–73. Boston, MA: Martinus Nijhoff Publishers, 1980.

Rosefielde, Steven, Masaaki Kuboniwa, Satoshi Mizobata, and Kumiko Haba, eds. *The Unwinding of the Globalist Dream.* Singapore: World Scientific Publishers, 2017.

Rosefielde, Steven and Danieal Quinn. *Democracy and Its Elected Enemies.* Cambridge, MA: Cambridge University Press, 2013.

Rosefielde, Steven, and Yiyi Liu. "Sovereign Debt Crises: Solidarity and Power." *Journal of Comparative Economic Studies* (2018).

Rosefielde, Steven, and Ralph W. Pfouts. *Inclusive Economic Theory.* Singapore: World Scientific Publishers, 2014.

Ross, Stephen. "The Economic Theory of Agency: The Principal's Problem." *American Economic Review* 63 (1973): 134–9.

Rozman, Gilbert, ed. *The East Asian Region: Confucian Heritage and Its Modern Adaption.* Princeton, NJ: Princeton University Press, 1991.

Rue, John E., Hoover Institution on War, Revolution, and Peace. *Mao Tse-tung in Opposition, 1927–1935*, 15. Palo Alto, CA: Stanford University Press, 1966.

Samuelson, Paul. "Evaluation of Real National Income." *Oxford Economic Papers* 2 (January 1950): 1–29.

———. *Foundations of Economic Analysis*. Cambridge, MA: Harvard University Press, 1947.

———. "The Problem of Integrability in Utility Theory." *Economica* 17 (1950): 255–85.

———. "Social Indifference Curves." *Quarterly Journal of Economics* 70 (February 1956): 1–22.

Scheffler, Samuel. *The Rejection of Consequentialism: A Philosophical Investigation of the Considerations Underlying Rival Moral Conceptions*. Oxford: Oxford University Press, 1994.

Seising, Rudolf. "The Fuzzification of Systems. The Genesis of Fuzzy Set Theory and Its Initial Applications—Developments up to the 1970s," In *Studies in Fuzziness and Soft Computing*, Vol. 216, Berlin: Springer, 2007.

Seligman, Martin. *Flourish: A New Understanding of Happiness and Well-being—And How to Achieve Them*. Boston, MA and London: Nicholas Brealey, 2011.

Sen, Amartya. "Personal Utilities and Public Judgements: Or What's Wrong with Welfare Economics." *Economic Journal* 89, no. 355 (1979): 537–88.

Shiller, Robert. *Irrational Exuberance*. Princeton, NJ: Princeton University Press, 2000.

Simon, Herbert. "A Behavioral Model of Rational Choice." *Quarterly Journal of Economics* 59 (1955): 99–118.

———. *Models of Bounded Rationality*. Cambridge, MA: Harvard University Press, 1982.

———. *Models of Man: Social and Rational-Mathematical Essays on Rational Human Behavior in a Social Setting*. New York: John Wiley, 1957.

———. "Theories of Decision Making in Economic Behavioral Science." *American Economic Review* 49 (1959): 99–118.

Smith, Adam. *The Wealth of Nations*. London: William Strahan, Thomas Cadell, 1776.

Solow, Robert. "Technical Change and the Aggregate Production Function." *Review of Economics and Statistics* 39, no. 3 (1957): 312–20.

Sommerstein, Alan. *Aristophanes' Ecclesiazusae*. London: Oxford University Press, 2007.

Stalin, Joseph. *Dialectical and Historical Materialism*. Moscow: Foreign Languages Publishing House, 1938.

State Council, People's Republic of China, *The Belt Road Initiative*, March 28, 2015. http://english.gov.cn/beltAndRoad.

Stigler, George. "The Development of Utility Theory." *Journal of Political Economy* 58, no. 4 (August 1950): 307–27.

Stiglitz, Joseph. *Globalization and Its Discontent*. New York: W.W. Norton, 2002.

Stiglitz, Joseph. *Making Globalization Work*. New York: W.W. Norton, 2006.

Suzumura, Kotaro, Kenneth Arrow, and Amartya Sen, eds. *Handbook of Social Choice and Welfare*. Vol. 1. Amsterdam, the Netherlands: Elsevier, 2002.

Swartz, Wendy. *Reading Tao Yuanming Shifting Paradigms of Historical Reception (427–1900)*. Cambridge, MA: Harvard University Press, 2008.

Taber, Charles. "The Interpretation of Foreign Policy Events: A Cognitive Process Theory." In *Problem Representation in Political Decision Making*, edited by Donald A. Sylvan, and James F. Voss. London: Cambridge University Press, 1998.

Talbott, Strobe. "America Abroad: The Birth of the Global Nation." *Time*, July 20, 1992.

Tsang, Steve. *The Vitality of Taiwan: Politics, Economics, Society and Culture*. London: Palgrave Macmillan, 2012.

Tselichtchev, Ivan, and Philippe Debroux. *Asia's Turning Point: An Introduction to Asia's Dynamic Economies at the Dawn of the New Century*. Singapore: John Wiley & Sons (Asia), 2009.

Van de Graaf, Jan. *Theoretical Welfare Economics*. Cambridge, MA: Cambridge University Press, 1957.

Van Ness, Peter. "Does China have What It Takes to Become a Global Hegemon?." *Wilson Quarterly*, Winter 2016.

Vogel, Ezra F. *Deng Xiaoping and the Transformation of China*. Cambridge, MA: Harvard University Press, 2011.

Weitzman, Martin. "The New Soviet Incentive Model." *Bell Journal of Economics* 7 (1976): 251–7.

———. "Prices versus Quantities." *Review of Economic Studies* 41 (1974): 477–91.

Wheelwright, Edward Lawrence, and Bruce McFarlane. *The Chinese Road to Socialism: Economics of the Cultural Revolution*. New York: Monthly Review Press, 1971.

Wildau, Gabriel, and Tom Mitchell. "China Income Inequality among World's Worst." *Financial Times*, January 14, 2016.

Williamson, Oliver. *The Economic Institutions of Capitalism: Firms, Markets and Relational Contracting*. New York: Free Press, 1985.

———. *Markets and Hierarchies*. New York: The Free Press, 1975.

———. *Mechanisms of Governance*. Oxford: Oxford University Press, 1996.

———. "The New Institutional Economics: Taking Stock, Looking Ahead." *Journal of Economic Literature* 38, no. 3 (September 2000): 595–613.

Wong, Christine. "Interpreting Rural Industrial Growth in the Post-Mao Period." *Modern China* 14, no. 1 (1988): 3–30.

Wright, Arthur. *Confucianism and Chinese Civilization*. Stanford, CA: Stanford University Press, 1961.

Xu, Gao. "State-Owned Enterprises in China: How Big Are They?" *World Bank Blog*, January 19, 2011.

Yu-Chen Lan, Jesse. "The Politics of Taiwanese Welfare State Transformation: Postindustrial Pressures, Regime Shifts and Social Policy Responses in the 1990s and Beyond." Working Paper, Department of Public Policy and Management, I-Shou University, Taiwan, 2009.

Zhang, Feng. "Beijing's Master Plan for the South China Sea." *Foreign Policy*, June 23, 2015.

INDEX